10 STEP DRAWING

Nature

Published in 2020 by Search Press Ltd.
Wellwood, North Farm Road
Tunbridge Wells
Kent, TN2 3DR

Reprinted 2020

This book is produced by
The Bright Press, an imprint of the Quarto Group,
The Old Brewery, 6 Blundell Street,
London N7 9BH, United Kingdom.
T (0)20 7700 6700
www.QuartoKnows.com

ISBN: 978-1-78221-855-5

Publisher: Mark Searle
Creative Director: James Evans
Managing Editor: Jacqui Sayers
Editor: Abbie Sharman
Design: JC Lanaway

Printed and bound in China

10 STEP DRAWING Nature

DRAW ⑥⓪ PLANTS & ANIMALS IN 10 EASY STEPS

MARY WOODIN

Search Press

Contents

>>> Meadows & Wetland

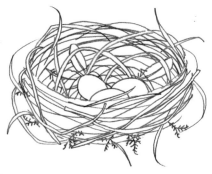

Forest

Coast

Introduction

In this book you will find 60 beautiful animal, plant and object illustrations that have been created in just ten simple steps. Whether it's a cheerful blue tit, a lost feather or a beautiful woodland plant, it's time to choose your favourite image and get drawing.

TACKLING DIFFERENT SHAPES

Plants and animals come in different shapes and sizes. Each drawing in this book begins with a simple shape or guide outline to begin with. The step-by-step instructions often also advise you to use further circles or other shape outlines as guides for placing heads and limbs, buds or individual petals and leaves. This will enable you to get the proportions right.

All of the drawings in this book involve lots of different shapes. Following the instructions and guides on what shape the elements should be will help you achieve the overall appearance of different plants and animals.

We have also provided a colour palette at the end of each finished drawing. Use this as a guide, but feel free to experiment and use your favourite shades for different flowers and plants or different colours for the animals' fur.

I hope you will enjoy creating the images in this book as much as I did. Drawing has never been easier!

How to use this book

BASIC EQUIPMENT

Paper: any paper will do, but using sketch paper will give you the best results.

Pencil, rubber and pencil sharpener: try different pencil grades and invest in a good-quality rubber.

Pen: for inking the final image. A medium or fine ink pen is best (ink is better than ballpoint because it dries quickly and is less likely to smudge).

Small ruler: this is optional, but you may find it useful for drawing guidelines.

FOLLOWING THE STEPS

Use pencil and follow each step. When you are happy with the image, draw over it in ink and leave it to dry. Then erase the underlying pencil. Finally, apply colour as you like.

COLOURING

Stay inside the lines and keep your pencils sharp so you have control in the smaller areas.

To achieve a lighter or darker shade, try layering the colour or pressing harder with your pencil.

Many plants and animals come in different colours and have different patterns, so once you're confident with where the shading should be on each one, why not try varying the colours you use?

You have several options when it comes to colouring your drawings – why not explore them all?

Pencils: this is the simplest option, and the one I have chosen for finishing the pictures in this book. A good set of coloured pencils, with about 24 shades, is really all you need.

Paint and brush: watercolour is probably easiest to work with for beginners, although using acrylic or oil means that you can paint over any mistakes. You'll need two or three brushes of different sizes, with at least one very fine brush.

Meadows
& Wetland

Blue tit

This small bird is a garden favourite and can be drawn using just a few simple shapes. Keep the colours vivid to bring your drawing to life.

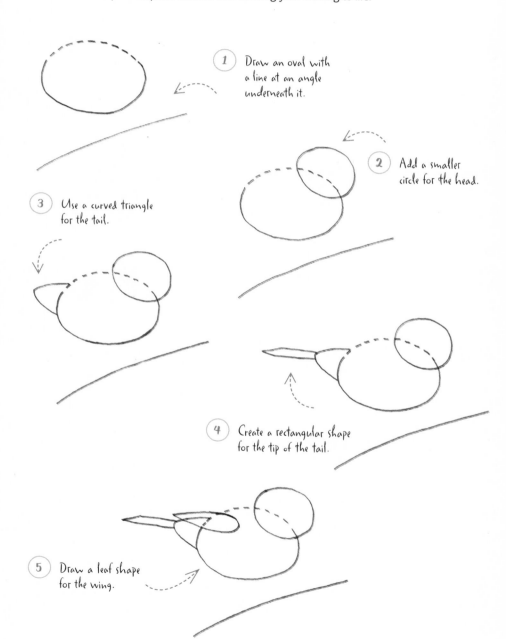

1 Draw an oval with a line at an angle underneath it.

2 Add a smaller circle for the head.

3 Use a curved triangle for the tail.

4 Create a rectangular shape for the tip of the tail.

5 Draw a leaf shape for the wing.

6 Use curved lines to connect the head to the body.

7 Add a small circle for the eye – leaving a small white dot in the middle. Create the beak.

8 Draw lines along the tip of the tail and the end of the wing. Add detail to the face.

9 Create the legs of the bird and draw the other side of the branch.

10 Use a bright yellow for its chest and a mixture of blues and greens for its back.

Borage

This Mediterranean plant is also known as a starflower,
so make sure to focus on its star-like flowers.

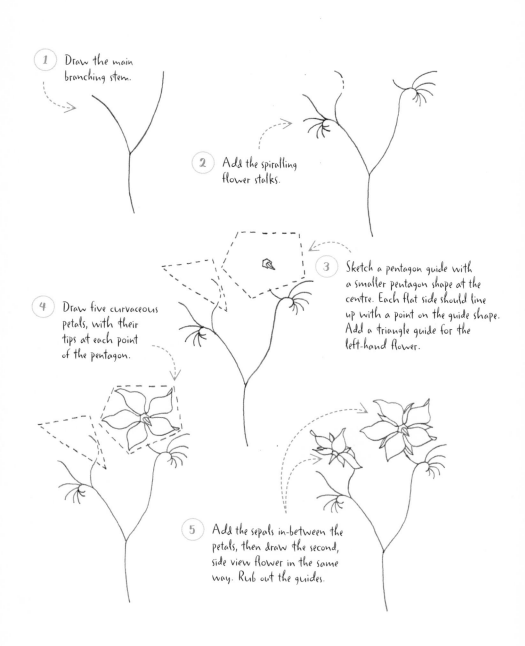

1. Draw the main branching stem.

2. Add the spiralling flower stalks.

3. Sketch a pentagon guide with a smaller pentagon shape at the centre. Each flat side should line up with a point on the guide shape. Add a triangle guide for the left-hand flower.

4. Draw five curvaceous petals, with their tips at each point of the pentagon.

5. Add the sepals in-between the petals, then draw the second, side view flower in the same way. Rub out the guides.

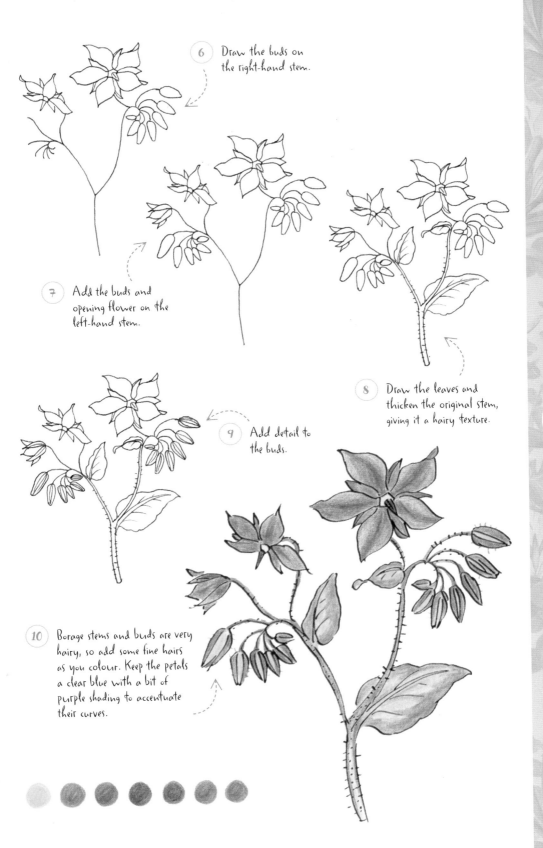

6 Draw the buds on the right-hand stem.

7 Add the buds and opening flower on the left-hand stem.

8 Draw the leaves and thicken the original stem, giving it a hairy texture.

9 Add detail to the buds.

10 Borage stems and buds are very hairy, so add some fine hairs as you colour. Keep the petals a clear blue with a bit of purple shading to accentuate their curves.

Blackberry

This delicious berry is the perfect addition to
the hedgerows of any meadow.

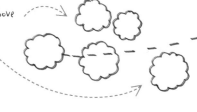

1. Draw a slightly curved horizontal line.
Create a cloud shape with about ten uneven
bumps at the end of the line. Leave a small
gap, then draw a second cloud crossing over
the line.

2. Add two more cloud shapes above
the guide and one below.

3. Draw three drupelets in
the centre of each berry.

4. Turn the guideline into
a prickly stem.

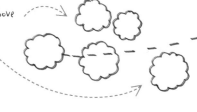

5. Working from the centre
outwards, fill the remaining
space in each berry with
drupelets. Towards the edge
they may only appear
as semicircles.

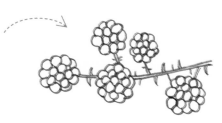

6　Draw a small circle surrounded by stamens for the blossom centre, and add sepals to the two blackberries above the stem.

7　Add the petals to the blossom.

8　Draw five lines for the stems of the leaves and add an outline to the left-hand leaves.

9　Working anticlockwise from the bottom, add the remaining overlapping leaves.

10　Leave highlights on the first three drupelets in each berry. Add texture to the leaves by adding lots of veining.

Dragonfly

Dragonflies are characterized by their elongated bodies and transparent wings.
Use colour on the wings but keep it light to preserve the transparent look.

1 Create a vertical guideline and draw squashed circles for the face and eyes.

2 Use a curved rectangle for the thorax.

3 Add the abdomen, making it about twice the length of the thorax. Rub out the guideline.

4 Draw a horizontal guideline across the thorax. Draw the top edges of the four wings, making them equal in length to the abdomen.

5 Add the lower edges of the wings.

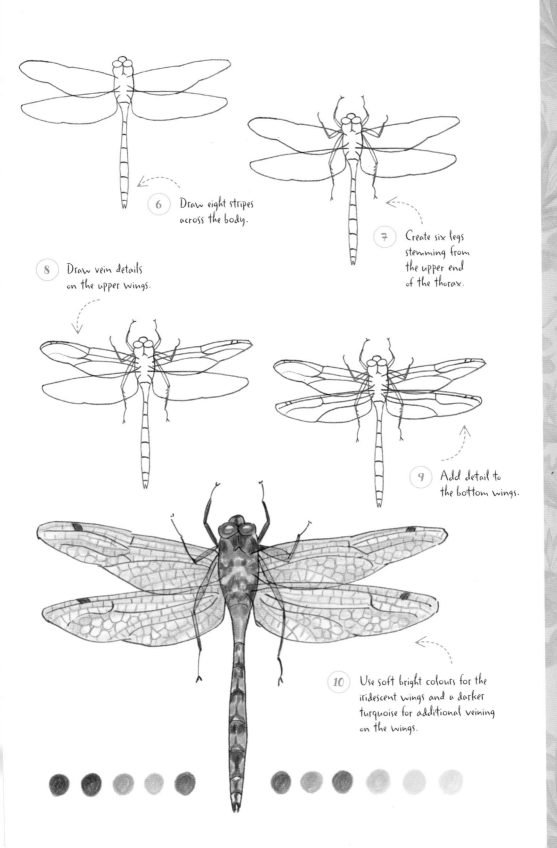

6 Draw eight stripes across the body.

7 Create six legs stemming from the upper end of the thorax.

8 Draw vein details on the upper wings.

9 Add detail to the bottom wings.

10 Use soft bright colours for the iridescent wings and a darker turquoise for additional veining on the wings.

Juniper

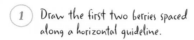

These evergreen plants are known for their needle-like leaves and blue berries.
Pay close attention to these elements to keep your drawing looking realistic.

1. Draw the first two berries spaced along a horizontal guideline.

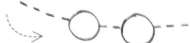

2. Above and below the gap between the berries, draw two more berries.

3. Hanging from the guideline, draw a fifth berry, with a side view.

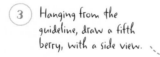

4. Add detail to the berries.

5. Draw the central twig along the original guideline and add side shoots.

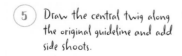

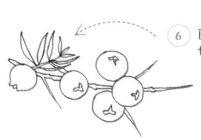

⑥ Draw needles, in bunches of three, along the first side shoot.

⑦ Add needles to the two lower shoots.

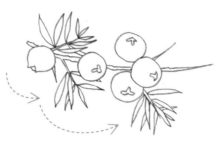

⑧ Continue adding needles to the two far right shoots.

⑨ Fill the central gap between the berries with a few more needles.

⑩ Use plenty of different greens for the needles to bring the drawing to life and leave a small white highlight on each berry.

Dandelion

This plant is well known for its bright yellow flower and fluffy seed.

① Draw a circle guide with a small oval in the centre.

② Add sepals to the central oval and a stalk emerging from the bottom.

③ Add six elliptical seeds, slightly overlapping the outer edge of the oval centre.

④ Give each seed a spine extending halfway to the outer circle.

⑤ Give each spine five or six 'wings'.

20

6 Add seven more seeds
   sitting on the edge of
   the oval centre and add
   spines extending as far
   as the tips of the first
   complete seeds.

3 4 5
2   6
1   7

7 Draw the wings
   for these seeds.

8 Fill the remaining space around
   the edge of the dotted circle
   with goblet-shaped wings
   attached to the central oval by
   long spines. Rub out the guide.

9 Draw a couple of
   individual seeds floating
   away on the breeze!

10 Over a pale-yellow base,
   increase the number of
   individual hairs that make up
   the wings in pale grey, to give
   the whole head a fluffy look.

Carolina wren

This American wren is usually found hiding in dense vegetation or forested areas. It has a bold white eyebrow and a tail that is the length of its body and often tilted upwards.

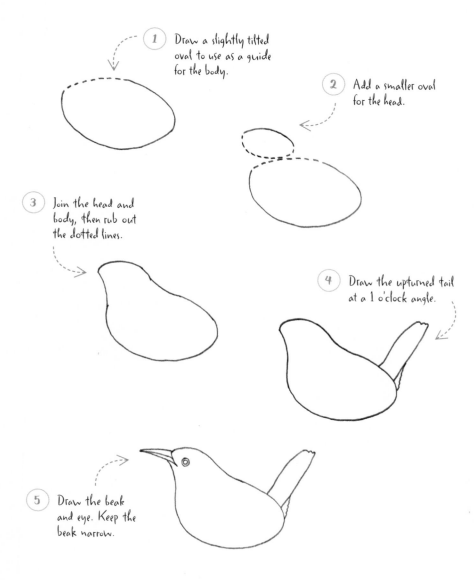

1. Draw a slightly tilted oval to use as a guide for the body.

2. Add a smaller oval for the head.

3. Join the head and body, then rub out the dotted lines.

4. Draw the upturned tail at a 1 o'clock angle.

5. Draw the beak and eye. Keep the beak narrow.

6) Add the lower line of the wing across the centre of the body.

7) Draw the legs, making sure to include the bend in the far leg.

8) Create the feet and branch.

9) Add detail to the feathers.

10) Create the characteristic horizontal stripes on the wing and tail feathers.

23

Herbs

With so many herbs to choose from, once you've mastered the basics you can experiment with different combinations.

1. Draw the three main leaf stems in a fan shape.

2. Add secondary stems.

3. Draw the wobbly outline of the bay leaf.

4. Sketch the smallest central sage leaves, giving them serrated edges.

5. Add the two larger leaves to the sage.

6 Tuck the largest central leaf in at the back of the other sage leaves. Draw tiny thyme leaves in bunches of four or five along the length of the left-hand thyme stem.

7 Do the same for the right-hand stem.

8 Finally, repeat this along the central stem.

9 Add vein details to the sage and bay leaves.

10 Use a wide variety of colours to create the different leaf textures.

Robin

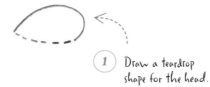

Starting with just a teardrop shape, you can create
this red-breasted garden favourite.

1   Draw a teardrop
    shape for the head.

2   Add the body and
    erase the bottom of
    the teardrop.

3   Create the
    foremost wing.

4   Add a circle for the eye
    and a slightly upward-
    slanting beak.

5   Draw the legs
    and rump.

6 Add the feet. They should have three toes pointing forward and one pointing back.

7 Add the tail and draw the furthest wing tip, emerging from behind the rump.

8 Draw parallel wing feathers.

9 Add detail around the red breast.

10 Create a feathered texture by layering colours in short strokes.

Clover

A bright touch for any meadow, use bright pinks
and greens to finish off your clover.

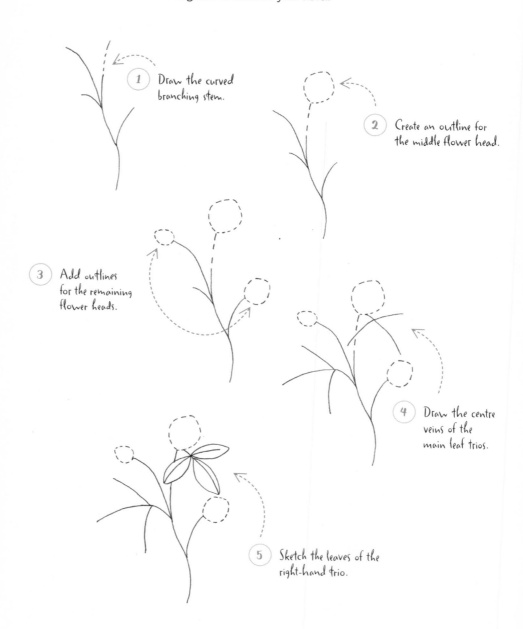

1. Draw the curved branching stem.

2. Create an outline for the middle flower head.

3. Add outlines for the remaining flower heads.

4. Draw the centre veins of the main leaf trios.

5. Sketch the leaves of the right-hand trio.

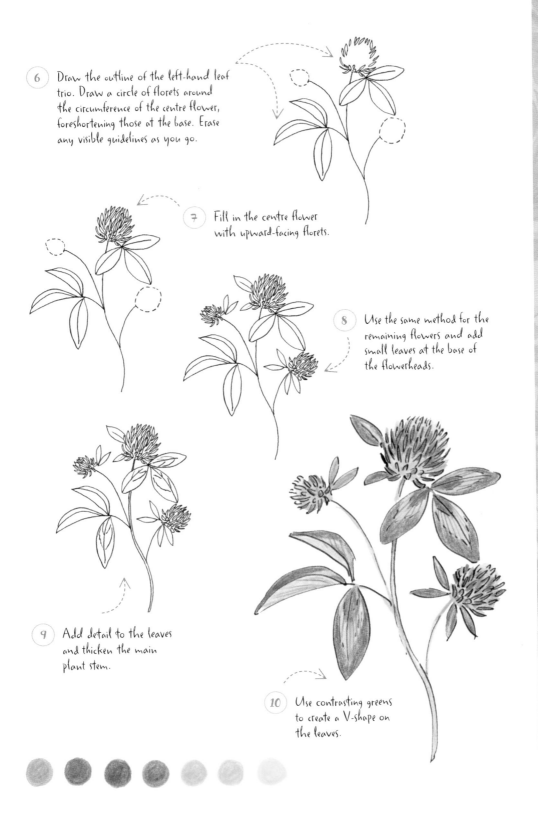

6 Draw the outline of the left-hand leaf
   trio. Draw a circle of florets around
   the circumference of the centre flower,
   foreshortening those at the base. Erase
   any visible guidelines as you go.

7 Fill in the centre flower
   with upward-facing florets.

8 Use the same method for the
   remaining flowers and add
   small leaves at the base of
   the flowerheads.

9 Add detail to the leaves
   and thicken the main
   plant stem.

10 Use contrasting greens
    to create a V-shape on
    the leaves.

Goldfinch

This brightly coloured finch has a vivid red face and distinct yellow wing patch,
which make it one of the prettiest of the garden birds.

1. Draw the head and a fairly fat beak.

2. Sketch a 45-degree dotted line through the centre of the headband, continuing the length of the bird, then draw the crossed-over wings.

3. Add the tail and then rub out the dotted guide.

4. Draw the breast.

5. Add the legs and twig.

(6) Wrap the toes around the twig.

(7) Draw the eye so that it sits level with the top half of the beak and add face markings. Draw two foreshortened blossom petals and anthers at the end of the twig.

(8) Draw wing feathers, then add three more petals to the blossom.

(9) Add tail feather details and a second blossom bud.

(10) Keep a flash of white on the tips of the wings and tail.

31

Olive

This bitter fruit makes a tasty treat. Create your own using simple shapes and deep colours.

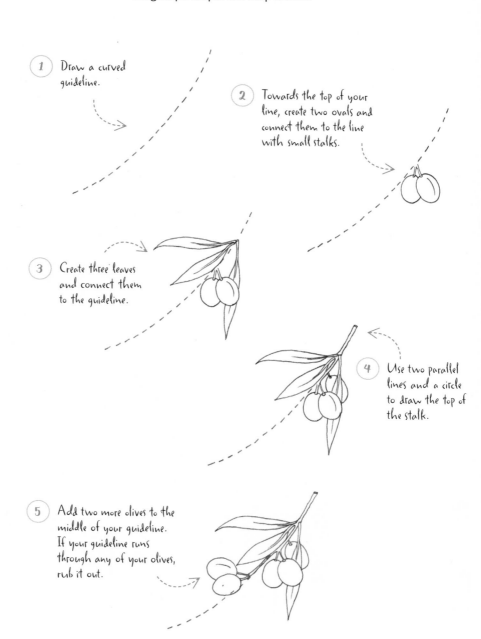

1. Draw a curved guideline.

2. Towards the top of your line, create two ovals and connect them to the line with small stalks.

3. Create three leaves and connect them to the guideline.

4. Use two parallel lines and a circle to draw the top of the stalk.

5. Add two more olives to the middle of your guideline. If your guideline runs through any of your olives, rub it out.

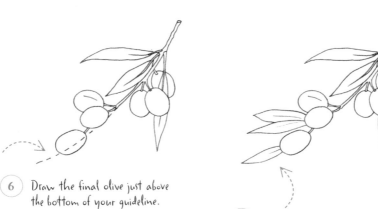

6 Draw the final olive just above the bottom of your guideline.

7 Create a leaf at the bottom of the guideline and add two more to the left side of the stalk. Rub out what is left of the guideline.

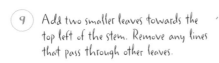

8 Fill out the right side of the stalk with additional leaves.

9 Add two smaller leaves towards the top left of the stem. Remove any lines that pass through other leaves.

10 Where the light hits the olives leave a small dot of white and use increasingly darker blues as you spiral outwards. Use a mixture of blues, greens and yellows to shade the leaves and stalk.

Barn owl

This majestic bird is the perfect addition to any night-time scene.
Add dark speckles to the feathers and soft brown shades to
the wings and back to make your owl pop.

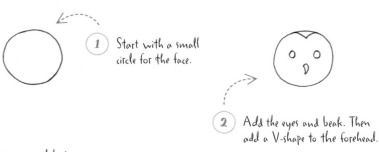

1. Start with a small circle for the face.

2. Add the eyes and beak. Then add a V-shape to the forehead.

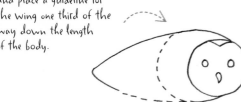

3. Draw a tapering oval body and place a guideline for the wing one third of the way down the length of the body.

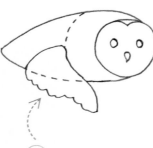

4. Draw the top of the closest wing.

5. Add a second layer of feathers to the wing.

6 Use long feathers for the final layer.

7 Add the far wing, starting from halfway down the face.

8 Draw the tail and the feet.

9 Give the feathers some detail.

10 Keep the owl's face pale, with a darker outer edge, and pay attention to the pattern of the darker spots on the outstretched wing feathers.

Pussy willow

Towards the end of winter, fuzzy nubs start to appear along the branches of pussy willows. These tufts resemble cats' paws and give the plant its name.

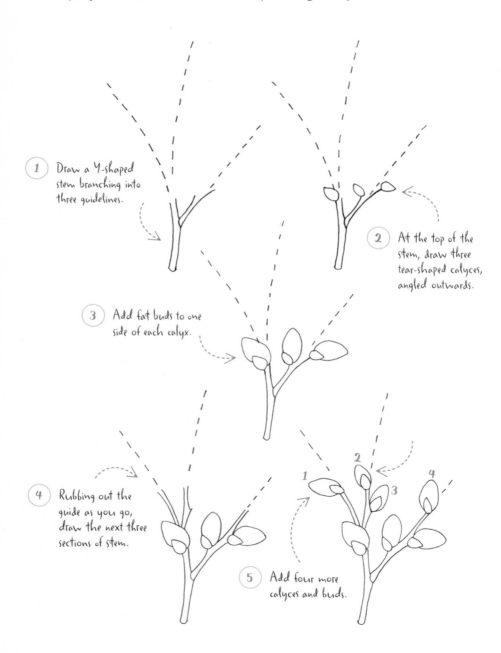

1) Draw a Y-shaped stem branching into three guidelines.

2) At the top of the stem, draw three tear-shaped calyces, angled outwards.

3) Add fat buds to one side of each calyx.

4) Rubbing out the guide as you go, draw the next three sections of stem.

5) Add four more calyces and buds.

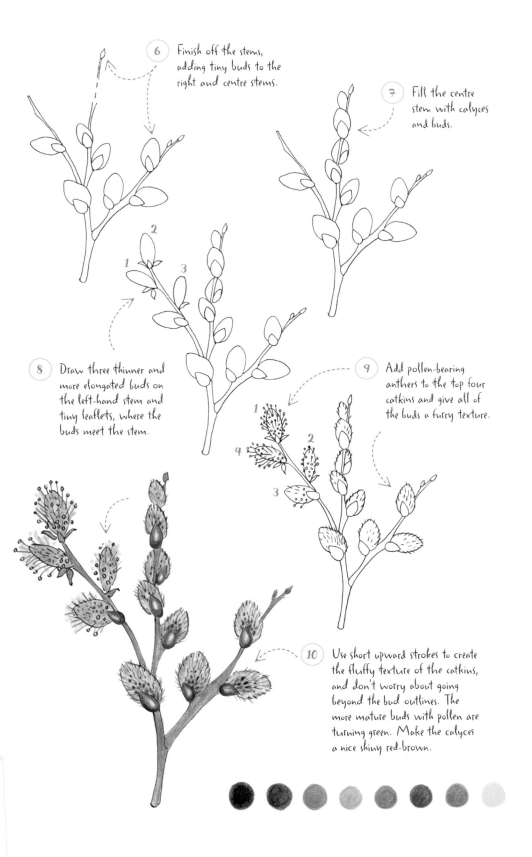

6 Finish off the stems, adding tiny buds to the right and centre stems.

7 Fill the centre stem with calyces and buds.

2
1
3

8 Draw three thinner and more elongated buds on the left-hand stem and tiny leaflets, where the buds meet the stem.

9 Add pollen-bearing anthers to the top four catkins and give all of the buds a furry texture.

1
2
4
3

10 Use short upward strokes to create the fluffy texture of the catkins, and don't worry about going beyond the bud outlines. The more mature buds with pollen are turning green. Make the calyces a nice shiny red-brown.

Camellia

Growing in hedgerows and gardens, these evergreens have thick, glossy
leaves and beautiful flowers which vary in colour, from white to red.

1. Draw a squashed circle guide, with an inverted cup shape in the centre.

2. Sketch a second, slightly off-centre oval guide. Draw the stamens to fill the cup shape.

3. Draw three petals, extending to the edge of the smaller oval.

4. Add the remaining three petals. Rub out the inner guide.

5. On the left side, create a second layer of overlapping petals. They should not quite reach the outer guide.

6 Starting with the centre petal, draw three more petals on the right side of the flower.

7 Finish with a final ring of petals extending to the outer guide. Rub out the guidelines.

8 Draw the flower stalk and central leaf veins.

9 Follow the shape of the central leaf veins to create the leaves.

10 Use pinks, fading to white at the very edges of the petals, and pale veining following the contour of the petals.

Californian poppy

This jazzy relative of the common poppy will give
a splash of colour to any meadow.

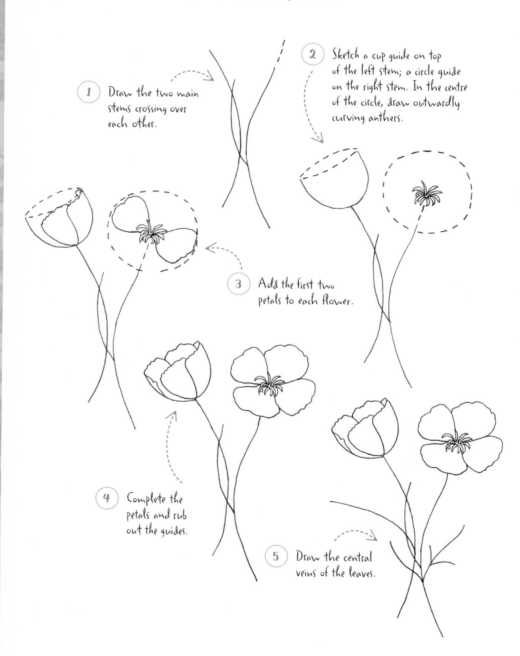

1 Draw the two main stems crossing over each other.

2 Sketch a cup guide on top of the left stem; a circle guide on the right stem. In the centre of the circle, draw outwardly curving anthers.

3 Add the first two petals to each flower.

4 Complete the petals and rub out the guides.

5 Draw the central veins of the leaves.

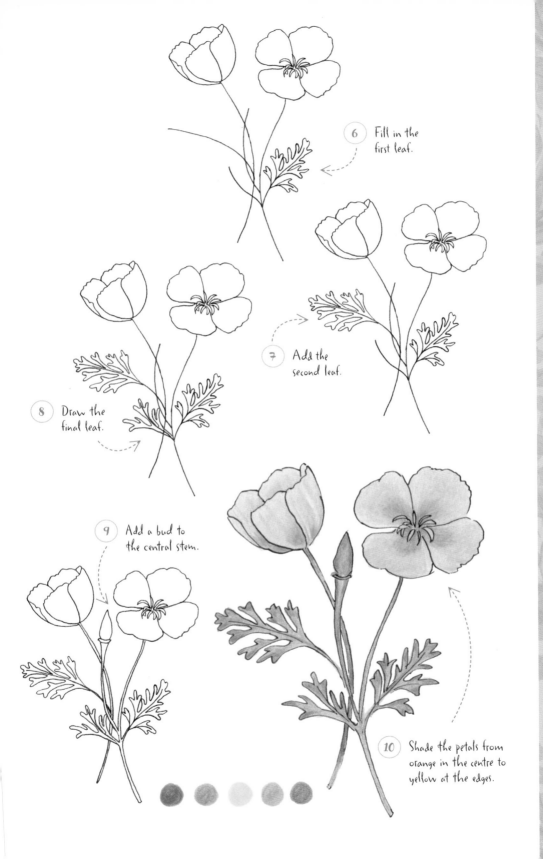

6 Fill in the first leaf.

7 Add the second leaf.

8 Draw the final leaf.

9 Add a bud to the central stem.

10 Shade the petals from orange in the centre to yellow at the edges.

Peacock butterfly

Butterflies are fun to draw because their wings display amazing colours and patterns. Why not try drawing different types of butterfly on your page?

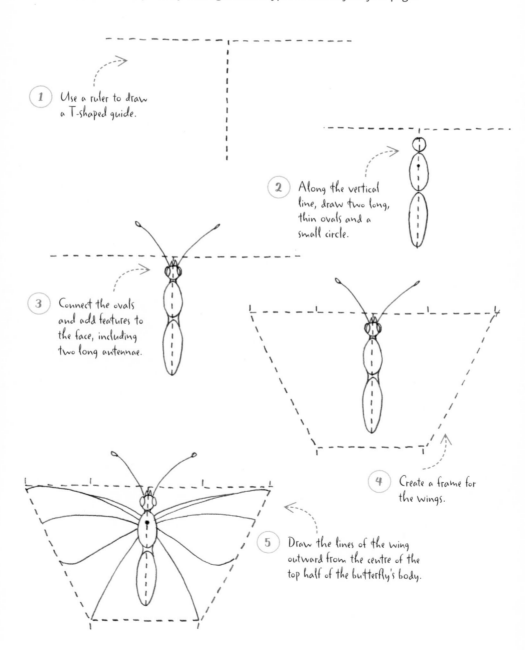

1. Use a ruler to draw a T-shaped guide.

2. Along the vertical line, draw two long, thin ovals and a small circle.

3. Connect the ovals and add features to the face, including two long antennae.

4. Create a frame for the wings.

5. Draw the lines of the wing outward from the centre of the top half of the butterfly's body.

6 Draw the edges of the wings, with curved lines connecting the different parts.

7 Rub out the guides and draw an inner line along the edge of the wings.

8 Add decorative circles to the wings, making sure they are symmetrical.

9 Decorate the wings further. Remember to repeat the shapes on both sides.

10 Follow our colour guide to create a Peacock butterfly, or experiment with your own selection of bright colours.

Strawberry

This brightly coloured fruit isn't just a garden favourite; it can also be found growing in the wild. Why not place yours in the hedgerow of a meadow?

(1) Draw a rough heart-shaped outline. For a more natural appearance, try not to make it look too symmetrical.

(2) Draw one upward-facing sepal and draw the stalk emerging from behind.

(3) Draw the rest of the sepals.

(4) Halfway down the strawberry, draw a horizontal row of small pips.

(5) In the lower half of the strawberry, add three more rows of pips. Place each pip midway between the two pips in the row above.

6 Repeat for the top half of the strawberry.

7 Draw three faint ovals as guides for the leaves.

8 Give the leaves serrated edges and add detail.

9 Add a small immature berry beneath the leaves. Remove the guides for the leaves.

10 To create the fresh shiny surface of the fruit, encircle the yellow pips with the darkest pink, then leave a white halo around each one before colouring the red body of the strawberry.

Mallard

A popular sight in ponds and lakes across town and country,
the much-loved mallard is our most familiar duck.
Make sure you capture the iconic green head.

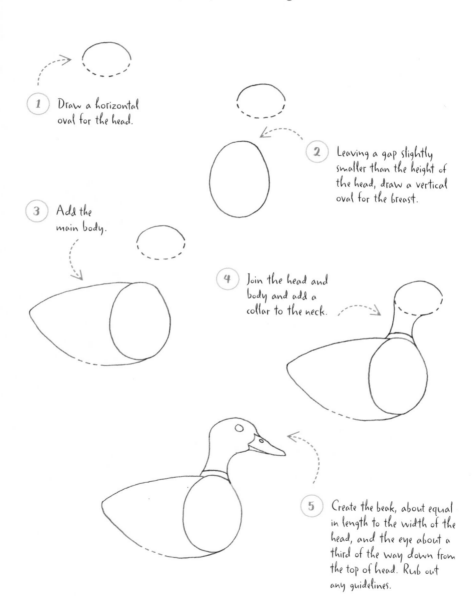

1. Draw a horizontal oval for the head.

2. Leaving a gap slightly smaller than the height of the head, draw a vertical oval for the breast.

3. Add the main body.

4. Join the head and body and add a collar to the neck.

5. Create the beak, about equal in length to the width of the head, and the eye about a third of the way down from the top of head. Rub out any guidelines.

6 Draw in the legs and feet, then rub out the guide at the top of the foremost leg.

7 Add detail to the feet, including claws and webbing.

8 Sketch in the wing.

47

9 Add tail feathers to the end of the body.

10 To achieve the sheen on the mallard's head, use a variety of greens and turquoise.

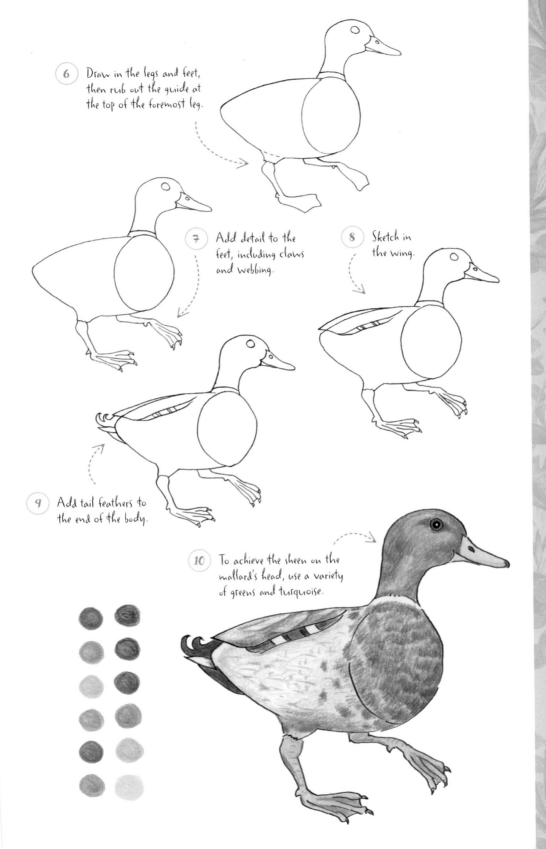

Dog rose

Master these simple steps to help you create this scrambling shrub,
which is at home in hedgerows, woodlands and grasslands.

1. Draw a circle guide and mark the centre with a small circle.

2. Divide the circle into five. Use the first guide to mark the centre of the first heart-shaped petal.

3. Add a petal to the guides either side of the first petal.

4. Draw the remaining two petals slightly overlapping each other. Rub out all the guides.

5. Sketch a circle of anthers in the centre.

6 Create the stem.

7 Add two leaves close to the end of the stem.

8 Draw the remaining leaves.

9 Add a tightly closed bud.

10 Keep the centre of the flower very pale, fading to darker pink at the edges.

Bumblebee

This cheerfully coloured insect can be spotted going from flower to flower.
These large, hairy bees are black with yellow banding.

1 Start by drawing a furry squashed circle.

2 Use circular shapes to create the head, then mark a highlight on the eye and add the antennae.

3 Draw the oval abdomen.

4 Sketch the top line of the wings, extending from the top of the body. The top wings should be equal in length to the body of the bee.

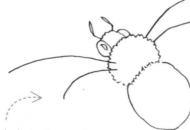

5 Draw the curved lower half of the wings.

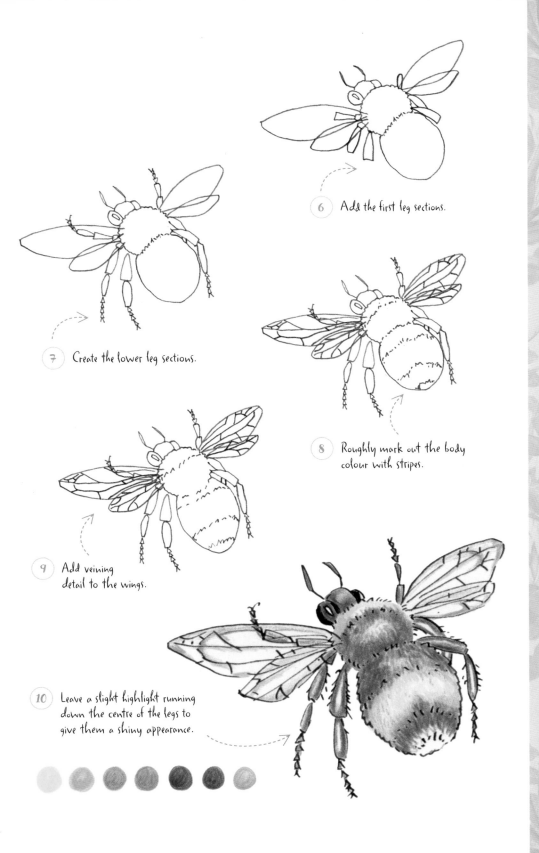

6 Add the first leg sections.

7 Create the lower leg sections.

8 Roughly mark out the body colour with stripes.

9 Add veining detail to the wings.

10 Leave a slight highlight running down the centre of the legs to give them a shiny appearance.

Cornflower

Taking its name from the cornfields it grew in as a weed,
this underappreciated wildflower is a joy to draw.

1. Draw single curved lines for the main stems.

2. Thicken the stems with a second line, widening at the top.

3. Draw a goblet shape at the top of the two main stems and sketch a lozenge-shaped guide on top.

4. Create two star-shaped florets at the bottom of each guide.

5. Fill the bottom halves of the guide with outwardly pointing floret petals.

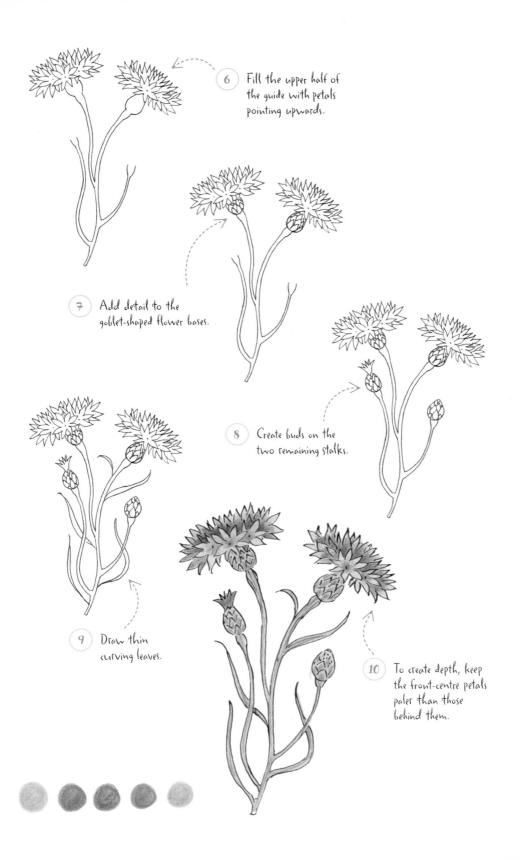

6 Fill the upper half of
   the guide with petals
   pointing upwards.

7 Add detail to the
   goblet-shaped flower bases.

8 Create buds on the
   two remaining stalks.

9 Draw thin
   curving leaves.

10 To create depth, keep
    the front-centre petals
    paler than those
    behind them.

Honeysuckle

Use a guide circle to create this delicate floral display. Follow our colour options or experiment with white, red, pink or orange.

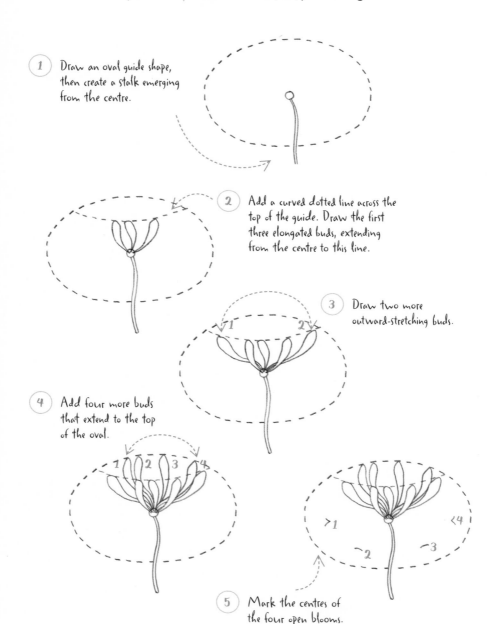

1 Draw an oval guide shape, then create a stalk emerging from the centre.

2 Add a curved dotted line across the top of the guide. Draw the first three elongated buds, extending from the centre to this line.

3 Draw two more outward-stretching buds.

4 Add four more buds that extend to the top of the oval.

5 Mark the centres of the four open blooms.

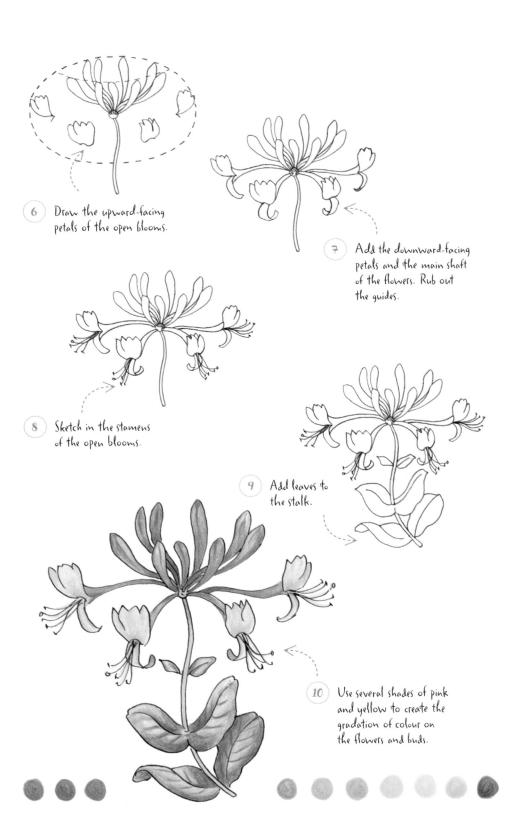

6 Draw the upward-facing petals of the open blooms.

7 Add the downward-facing petals and the main shaft of the flowers. Rub out the guides.

8 Sketch in the stamens of the open blooms.

9 Add leaves to the stalk.

10 Use several shades of pink and yellow to create the gradation of colour on the flowers and buds.

Harvest mouse

Typically found in fields of cereal crops or tall ground vegetation,
this tiny mouse is the perfect creature to add to your meadow.

1. Draw two long stems and create a guideline halfway up.

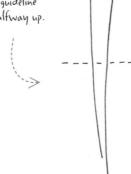

2. Draw an oval over the stems, with the lower portion just crossing over the guideline. Rub out the guide.

3. Add a curved shape for the mouse's head.

4. Sketch the eye, mouth, nose and ear. Use guides to help with positioning if needed.

5. Thicken the stem of the corn and add three leaf shapes to the top of the first one.

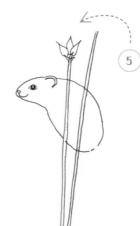

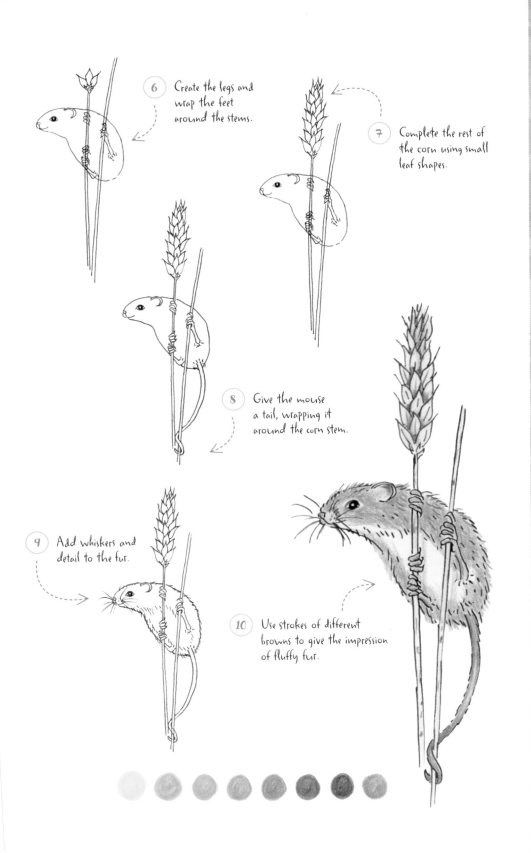

6 Create the legs and wrap the feet around the stems.

7 Complete the rest of the corn using small leaf shapes.

8 Give the mouse a tail, wrapping it around the corn stem.

9 Add whiskers and detail to the fur.

10 Use strokes of different browns to give the impression of fluffy fur.

Columbine

Found in meadows and woodlands, these plants are known
for the spurred petals of their flowers.

1. Draw the central veins of
   the three leaves and surround
   them with a rough
   lozenge-shaped guide.

2. Add curving flower
   stems coming from the
   right side of the lozenge.

3. Draw a cluster of five
   upward spurs on the
   left-hand flower stalk.

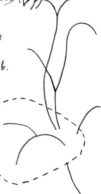

4. Add four fanned-
   out, pointed petals.

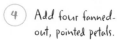

5. Finish the flower by
   adding the blades
   and stamens.

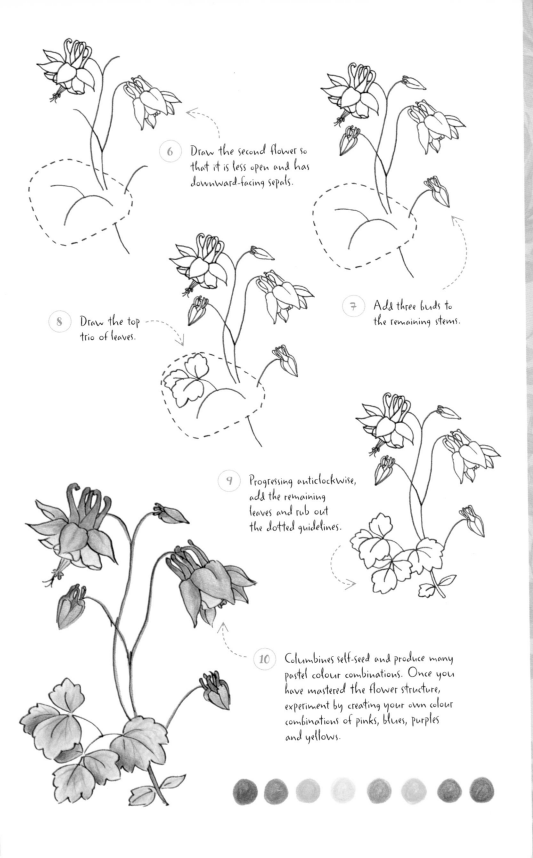

6 Draw the second flower so
   that it is less open and has
   downward-facing sepals.

8 Draw the top
   trio of leaves.

7 Add three buds to
   the remaining stems.

9 Progressing anticlockwise,
   add the remaining
   leaves and rub out
   the dotted guidelines.

10 Columbines self-seed and produce many
    pastel colour combinations. Once you
    have mastered the flower structure,
    experiment by creating your own colour
    combinations of pinks, blues, purples
    and yellows.

Bull reed

Found near lakes and riversides, this plant is the
perfect addition to any lakeland scene.

1 Draw three guide stems.
   The centre stem should
   extend furthest at the
   top and bottom.

2 Add the
   flower heads.

3 Draw the first
   two leaf blades
   on the centre stem.

4 Add two leaves
   to the left stem,
   behind the first
   two leaves.

5 Sketch two more
   leaves at the base
   of the centre stem.

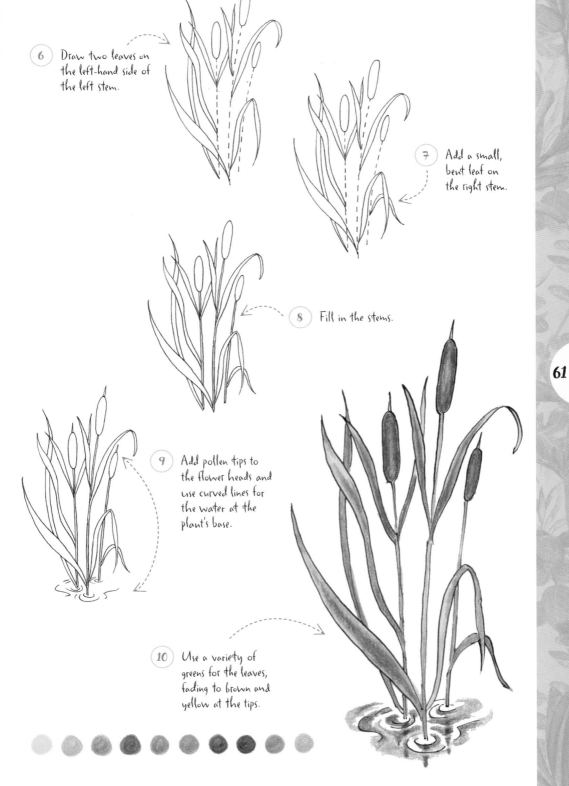

6. Draw two leaves on the left-hand side of the left stem.

7. Add a small, bent leaf on the right stem.

8. Fill in the stems.

9. Add pollen tips to the flower heads and use curved lines for the water at the plant's base.

10. Use a variety of greens for the leaves, fading to brown and yellow at the tips.

Forest

Bird's nest

Create a cosy home for your favourite bird
using simple lines and shapes.

1. Sketch a dotted oval
with an inner arc,
extending halfway
up the oval.

2. Draw three overlapping
eggs emerging from
the base line.

3. In the inner arc, draw
crisscrossing lines roughly
following the direction
of the arc.

4. Add four thicker,
free-flowing strands in
the upper half of the
oval. Add a bowl-shaped
guideline for the base of
the nest.

5. Draw a few patches of moss
along the base and add
three small feathers to the
lining of the nest.

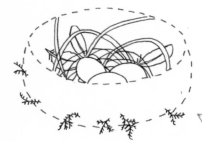

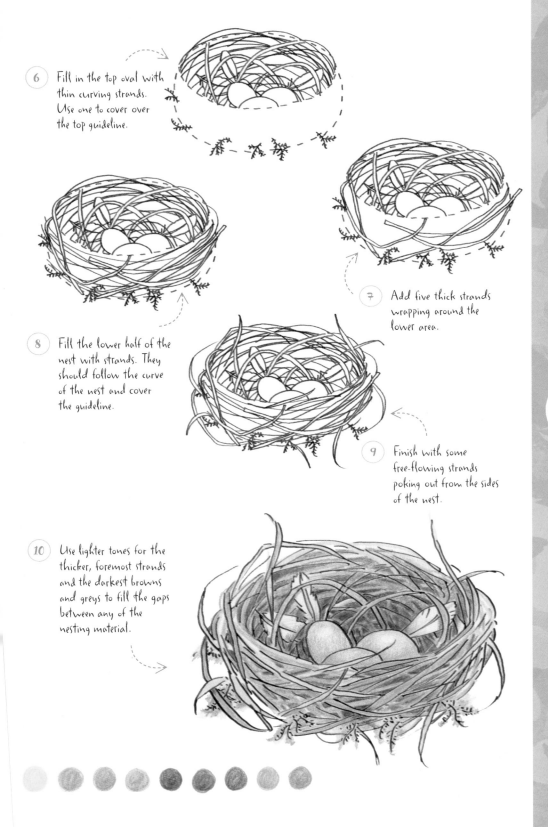

6 Fill in the top oval with thin curving strands. Use one to cover over the top guideline.

7 Add five thick strands wrapping around the lower area.

8 Fill the lower half of the nest with strands. They should follow the curve of the nest and cover the guideline.

9 Finish with some free-flowing strands poking out from the sides of the nest.

10 Use lighter tones for the thicker, foremost strands and the darkest browns and greys to fill the gaps between any of the nesting material.

Hummingbird

These active little birds spend nearly all of their time in the air, visiting nectar-filled flowers. Once you've drawn yours, try adding flowers around it.

1. Draw an eye shape.

2. Add a leaf shape just underneath the eye shape.

3. Draw a long, thin beak and add a circle for the eye.

4. Create a long oval for the body.

5. Add a rounded triangle at the bottom of the body.

7 Position triangular shapes on the bird's back for the base of the wings.

6 Draw the tail feathers sticking out from the triangle.

8 From the triangle wing shapes, draw the rest of the wings, with a serrated edge.

9 Add detail to the face, breast and wing and tail feathers.

10 Use bright colours with white flecks to give your hummingbird a reflective finish.

Hazel catkins

These unusual yellow flowers are actually made up of hundreds
of individual flowers arranged on a dangling stem.

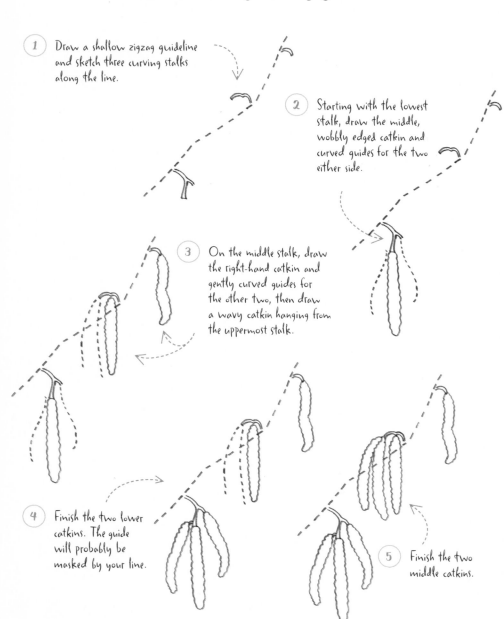

1. Draw a shallow zigzag guideline and sketch three curving stalks along the line.

2. Starting with the lowest stalk, draw the middle, wobbly edged catkin and curved guides for the two either side.

3. On the middle stalk, draw the right-hand catkin and gently curved guides for the other two, then draw a wavy catkin hanging from the uppermost stalk.

4. Finish the two lower catkins. The guide will probably be masked by your line.

5. Finish the two middle catkins.

6 Draw tiny curve-topped triangles down the centre of all the catkins.

7 Fill in the sides with horizontally topped triangles.

8 Draw the stem, thicker at the bottom and tapering as it reaches the top.

9 Add the female buds.

10 Give the catkins a central yellow core, linking the triangular sections, and give the female buds bright red styles.

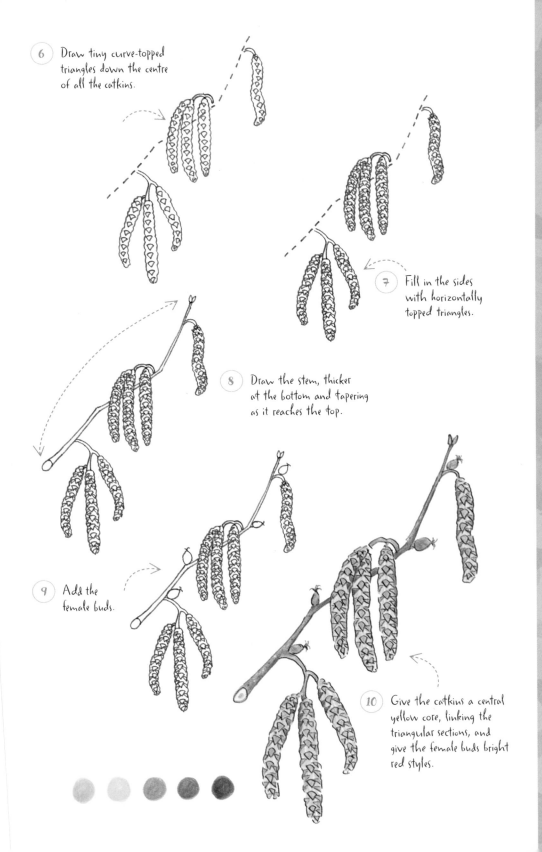

Northern cardinal

These colourful birds are also known as the redbird, so don't
be afraid to use a bright red to make the feathers bold.

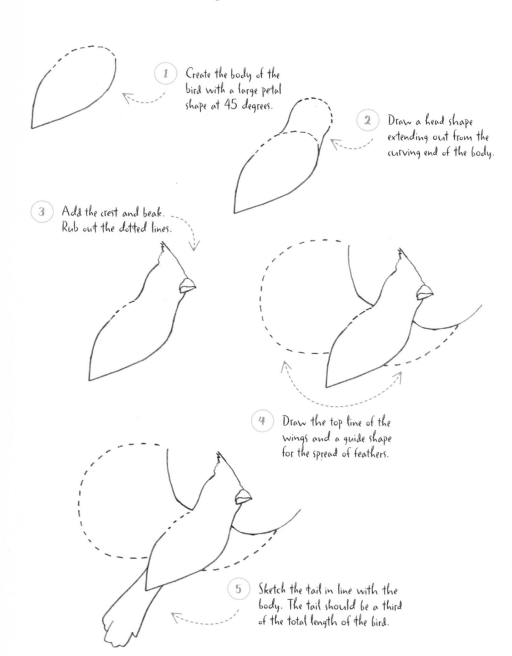

1. Create the body of the bird with a large petal shape at 45 degrees.

2. Draw a head shape extending out from the curving end of the body.

3. Add the crest and beak. Rub out the dotted lines.

4. Draw the top line of the wings and a guide shape for the spread of feathers.

5. Sketch the tail in line with the body. The tail should be a third of the total length of the bird.

6 Create a zigzag line across the top of the left wing, then draw the lower edge of the main feathers fanning out to the dotted guideline. Rub out the guide.

7 Finish creating the feathers on the left wing.

8 Use a zigzag line to create the top of the right wing, then draw the feathers curving out from this. Rub out the guide.

9 Add the feet. Then add detail to the face and tail.

10 Keep the underside of the wings paler than the body; just use darker tones where the feathers overlap.

Pine cone

A common sight on any woodland floor, pine cones are the woody, conical-shaped fruit of the pine tree. Draw your own by starting with a simple egg shape.

1. Draw an egg-shaped guide.

2. Add five faint horizontal lines in the lower third.

3. Add four faint diagonal lines in the top two thirds, then rub out the guide.

4. Draw three rows of diamond-shaped scales at the bottom of the cone.

5. Create one more layer of scales, adding their vertical sides.

6. Using the lines as a guide, add the next two rows of scales.

7. Add the tops to the final rows of scales.

8. Attach the tops of the scales to their vertical sides.

9. Fill in spaces at the edges with side view scales to complete the overall shape, then add the stalk.

10. Keep the tips of the scales pale and use a dark brown to create depth towards the centre of the cone.

Walnut

Walnuts are the stone fruits of the walnut tree and are often found on the woodland floor. Try using them on the ground in your woodland drawing.

1. Draw an oval with a point at one end. Add a second curve on the lower edge.

2. Create a second wider oval with the point to the lower right and add a circle at the back.

3. Draw a single line just inside the top edge of the right-hand nut, then a wiggly line either side.

4. Draw a wavy line just inside the rim of the halved nut.

5. Add the walnut half.

6. Draw a knobbly texture on the right-hand walnut and add dots to the furthest, 'green' walnut.

7. Create the main leaf stem running horizontally and add secondary stems.

8. Sketch the leaves along the secondary stems.

9. Add regularly spaced vein details to the leaves.

10. Leave tiny white specks on the surface of the 'green' walnut and colour this in green. Make sure the leaf veins are yellow and uniform.

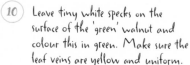

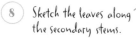

Chipmunk

With their big eyes, bushy tails, striped backs and chubby cheeks, these cheeky rodents are easy to recognize as they dart about in woodlands.

(1) Draw a wedge shape for the head.

(2) Add the ears, eyes and nose.

(3) Draw the filled cheeks.

(4) Draw the foremost arm.

(5) Add the rounded body.

(6) Draw the front paws clutching a nut.

(7) Draw five-toed feet, with the two outer toes shorter than the middle three.

(8) Sketch the tail with short strokes.

(9) Add details to the eye and draw markings for colour on the face and back.

(10) Use different shades of brown to highlight the characteristic striped markings.

Acorn

This nut of the oak tree is a favourite of squirrels everywhere and is a must for any woodland drawing, with its simple shape and elegant leaves.

(1) Draw two guide ovals at 90 degrees to one another.

(2) Covering the upper third of each oval, draw two cups which are slightly wider than the ovals. Rub out the guides.

(3) Draw the gently curving central leaf veins at 90 degrees to one another.

(4) Draw faint diagonal lines curving around the acorn cups.

(5) On the cups, add diagonal lines in the opposite direction to form a diamond grid.

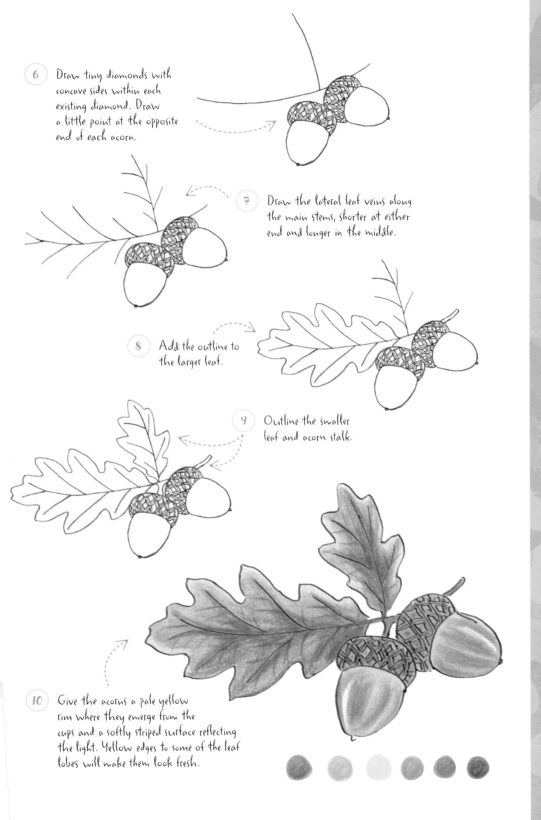

6 Draw tiny diamonds with concave sides within each existing diamond. Draw a little point at the opposite end of each acorn.

7 Draw the lateral leaf veins along the main stems, shorter at either end and longer in the middle.

8 Add the outline to the larger leaf.

9 Outline the smaller leaf and acorn stalk.

10 Give the acorns a pale yellow rim where they emerge from the cups and a softly striped surface reflecting the light. Yellow edges to some of the leaf lobes will make them look fresh.

Deer

Follow these simple steps to draw this graceful animal in your woodland scene. Make sure the antlers are symmetrical.

1. Draw a wedge-shaped head and jawline.

2. Add the neck.

3. Create the front of the body.

4. Draw the hind legs, overlapping slightly at the knees, and connect these to the rest of the body. Rub out the guides.

5. Add front legs that are parallel to one another.

6. Draw the ears, nose and eye. The centre of the eye should be level with where the lower edge of the ears meet the head.

7. Draw symmetrical antlers in a goblet shape. They should have five prongs on each side.

8. Sketch in the hooves.

9. Add the tail and white markings on the rump.

10. Keep the rump a distinctive white colour, then layer browns and greys to create a mottled texture of fur on the rest of the body.

Hawthorn

Also known as the May tree, due to its flowering period, this tree or shrub is characterized by its dense, thorny habit. Look out for its deeply lobed leaves, spiny twigs and haws (berries).

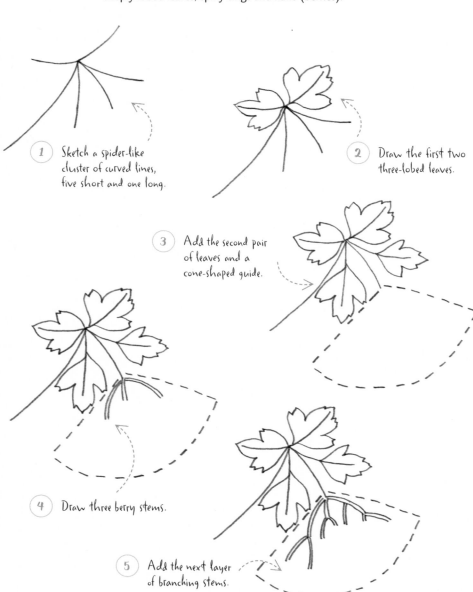

1 Sketch a spider-like cluster of curved lines, five short and one long.

2 Draw the first two three-lobed leaves.

3 Add the second pair of leaves and a cone-shaped guide.

4 Draw three berry stems.

5 Add the next layer of branching stems.

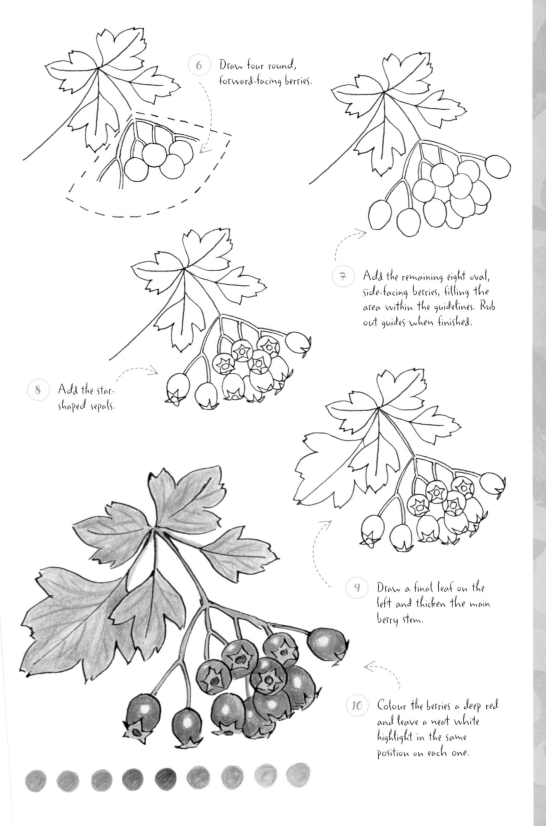

6 Draw four round, forward-facing berries.

7 Add the remaining eight oval, side-facing berries, filling the area within the guidelines. Rub out guides when finished.

8 Add the star-shaped sepals.

9 Draw a final leaf on the left and thicken the main berry stem.

10 Colour the berries a deep red and leave a neat white highlight in the same position on each one.

Hedgehog

If attacked, hedgehogs curl into a prickly ball that deters most predators.
Remember to give your hedgehogs a coat of stiff, sharp spines.

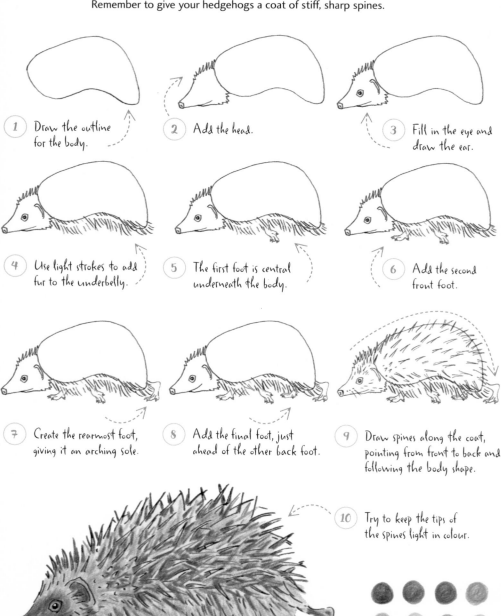

1. Draw the outline for the body.

2. Add the head.

3. Fill in the eye and draw the ear.

4. Use light strokes to add fur to the underbelly.

5. The first foot is central underneath the body.

6. Add the second front foot.

7. Create the rearmost foot, giving it an arching sole.

8. Add the final foot, just ahead of the other back foot.

9. Draw spines along the coat, pointing from front to back and following the body shape.

10. Try to keep the tips of the spines light in colour.

Frog

Once you've finished your woodland-variety frog, why not try creating
one from the rainforest and changing the colours to vivid shades.

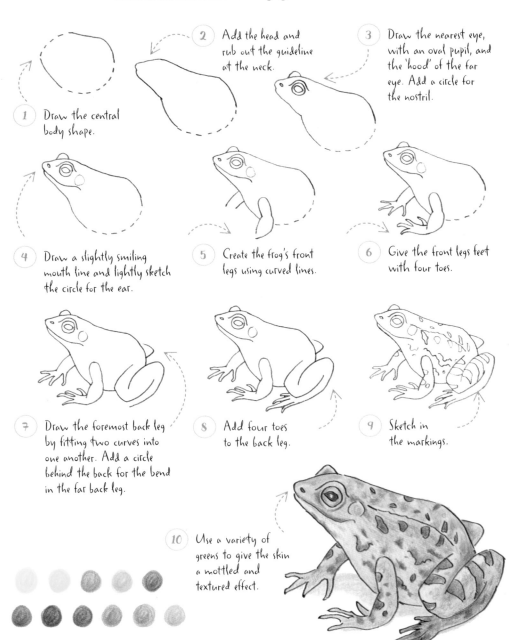

1) Draw the central body shape.

2) Add the head and rub out the guideline at the neck.

3) Draw the nearest eye, with an oval pupil, and the 'hood' of the far eye. Add a circle for the nostril.

4) Draw a slightly smiling mouth line and lightly sketch the circle for the ear.

5) Create the frog's front legs using curved lines.

6) Give the front legs feet with four toes.

7) Draw the foremost back leg by fitting two curves into one another. Add a circle behind the back for the bend in the far back leg.

8) Add four toes to the back leg.

9) Sketch in the markings.

10) Use a variety of greens to give the skin a mottled and textured effect.

Bee orchid

This look-alike is pollinated by the male bees that it attracts with its female bee pattern. Try drawing a male bee next to yours.

1. Draw the main stem with a triangular-shaped guide centred just to the right and a diamond centred to the left.

2. In the centre of the shapes, draw the hood and lips of the flowers.

3. Add the horizontal sepals.

4. Draw the vertical sepals.

5. Rub out the guides and add detail to the horizontal sepals.

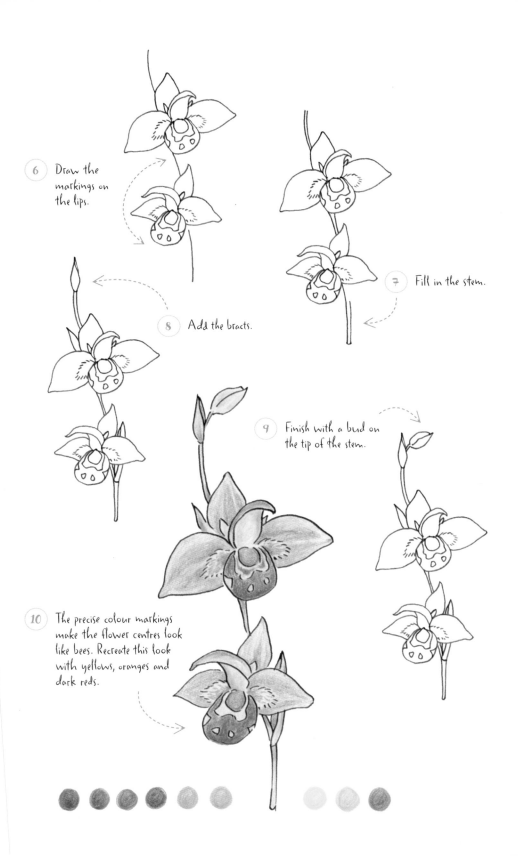

6 Draw the markings on the lips.

7 Fill in the stem.

8 Add the bracts.

9 Finish with a bud on the tip of the stem.

10 The precise colour markings make the flower centres look like bees. Recreate this look with yellows, oranges and dark reds.

Fern

Ferns are the perfect foliage plants to add softness to the lower, shadier areas of your woodland scene.

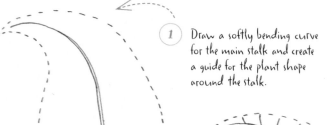

1. Draw a softly bending curve for the main stalk and create a guide for the plant shape around the stalk.

2. Add guidelines for leaflets fanning out from the stalk.

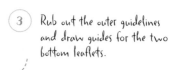

3. Rub out the outer guidelines and draw guides for the two bottom leaflets.

4. Draw the individual sub-leaflets along the length of the two lower leaflets.

5. Using the same process, draw the next two leaflets.

6 Working up the stem in the same way, fill in the leaflets.

7 Complete the frond, use fewer leaflets towards the top.

8 Draw a spiralling line for the fiddlehead (uncurling frond).

9 Add some emerging leaflets along the length of the fiddlehead.

10 Use darker greens in the centre of the leaflets, fading to pale green at the edges.

Maple

These trees are easily recognizable with their palmate leaves and distinctive winged fruits. Use autumn colours for maximum impact.

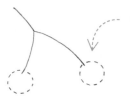

(1) Draw a stem with two branches, with a guide circle at the end of each branch.

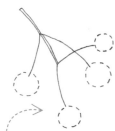

(2) Thicken the main stem and draw two more branches ending in circles.

(3) From the end of the lowest branch, draw a fan of five lines, the shortest being a quarter of the length of the longest. Do the same for the top right branch.

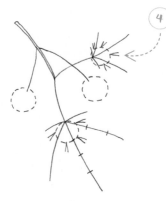

(4) Between each fan line, draw slim V-shaped indentations, sitting on the dotted circle.

(5) Draw the central serrated lobe on each leaf.

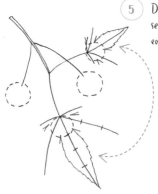

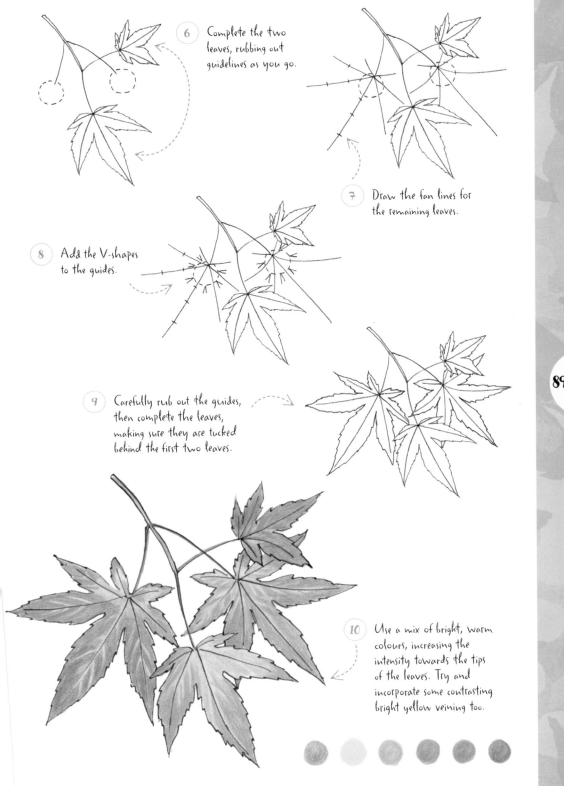

6 Complete the two leaves, rubbing out guidelines as you go.

7 Draw the fan lines for the remaining leaves.

8 Add the V-shapes to the guides.

9 Carefully rub out the guides, then complete the leaves, making sure they are tucked behind the first two leaves.

10 Use a mix of bright, warm colours, increasing the intensity towards the tips of the leaves. Try and incorporate some contrasting bright yellow veining too.

Raccoon

With its dark rimmed eyes, the raccoon is the robber of the animal world, but how to draw this sneaky chap doesn't need to escape you.

1 Draw the furry outline of the head.

2 Add the ears.

3 Draw the front leg coming down from the middle of the chin.

4 Add the second leg to the left of the first.

5 Draw the back leg.

6 Give the racoon a fat tail.

7 Add the remaining leg, then draw the feet.

8 Draw the face, with small round eyes about two fifths up from the chin. Mark the distinct areas of black and white on the face.

9 Add strokes to indicate the fur, especially the stripes on the tail.

10 Follow the curves of the body with dark pencil strokes to create the long thick fur. Keep distinct areas of black and white on the face.

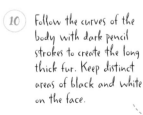

Violet

Create this wild favourite by giving it heart-shaped leaves and purple-blue flowers.

1. Draw a dome-shaped guide and, starting slightly off-centre at the base, draw the five main curvaceous stems.

2. Fill out the stems.

3. Draw two heart-shaped leaves attached to the two outer stems.

4. Draw the lower three petals on two of the stems.

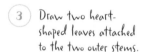

5. Add the top two petals on the right-hand flower.

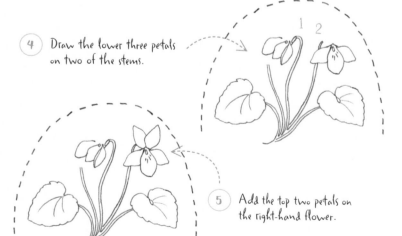

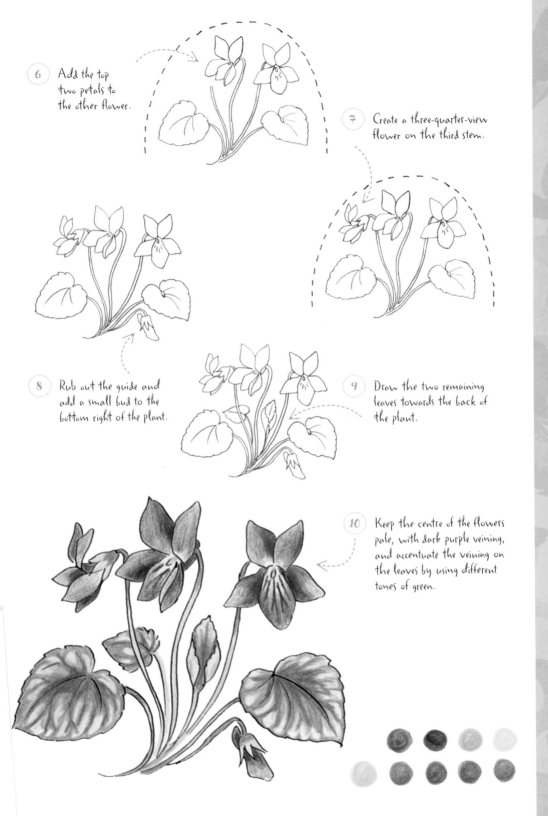

6 Add the top two petals to the other flower.

7 Create a three-quarter-view flower on the third stem.

8 Rub out the guide and add a small bud to the bottom right of the plant.

9 Draw the two remaining leaves towards the back of the plant.

10 Keep the centre of the flowers pale, with dark purple veining, and accentuate the veining on the leaves by using different tones of green.

93

Black bear

Black bears are excellent tree climbers and typically live in forests. Their coats can be black, blue-grey or blue-black, brown or cinnamon coloured.

(1) Draw a circle for the head and mark the centre with a dot.

(2) Add the muzzle and upright rounded ears. Then rub out the guidelines.

(3) Draw a curved line for the shoulder and disappearing leg.

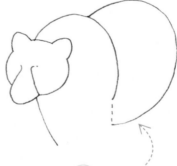

(4) Create a second curve for the back.

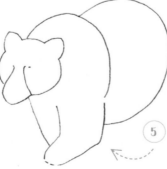

(5) Draw the front leg.

6 Add the back legs.

7 Draw the two visible paws.

8 Add detail to the face with its eyes, nose and fur.

9 Add the claws to the feet and indicate fur detail.

10 Layer dark grey, brown, indigo and black for the fur. Use short strokes following the curves of the body.

Toadstool

Create your own image of a toadstool that has a fruiting body
with a stalk and a cap by following these simple steps.

1. Draw two guides in an open V-shape. Extending halfway down the right-hand guideline, draw an oval shape with the top slightly more rounded than the bottom.

2. Divide this oval horizontally into thirds. Along the top third, draw a horizontal line that curves down so it is level with the bottom third as it reaches the outside edges.

3. Draw a gently curved stalk, following the vertical guideline.

4. Starting at the lower third level, draw a second oval on the left, coming halfway down its vertical guideline.

5. Add a bulbous stalk. Erase all visible guidelines.

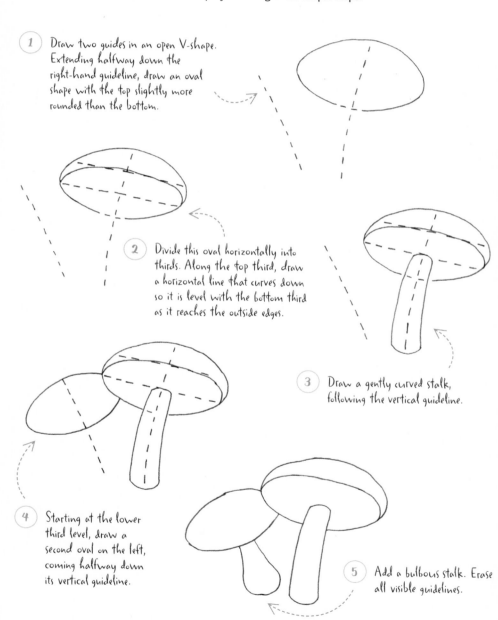

6 Draw the underside gills of the right-hand toadstool with widely spaced lines.

7 Fill in the spaces with two or three more lines per gap.

8 Draw irregular spots on the top surface of both fungi.

9 Add some frills around the stalks and some blades of grass at their bases.

10 Use two or three different reds for the tops of the toadstools and try to leave a paler highlight to give it a sheen. Keep the underside and stalks pale.

Lily of the valley

This delicate-looking plant is sweetly scented and highly poisonous.
It is native throughout the Northern Hemisphere in Asia and Europe.

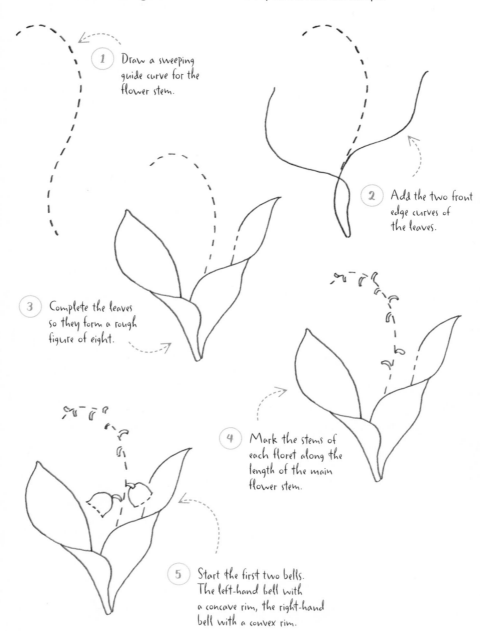

1. Draw a sweeping guide curve for the flower stem.

2. Add the two front edge curves of the leaves.

3. Complete the leaves so they form a rough figure of eight.

4. Mark the stems of each floret along the length of the main flower stem.

5. Start the first two bells. The left-hand bell with a concave rim, the right-hand bell with a convex rim.

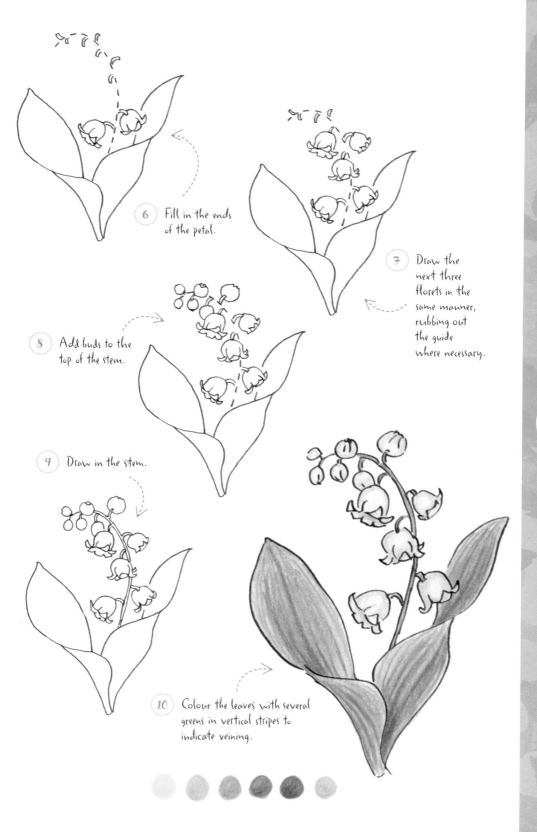

6 Fill in the ends of the petal.

7 Draw the next three florets in the same manner, rubbing out the guide where necessary.

8 Add buds to the top of the stem.

9 Draw in the stem.

10 Colour the leaves with several greens in vertical stripes to indicate veining.

Feather

With so many different birds, the variety of feathers you could draw is amazing. Try this one before moving on to feathers of different sizes, textures and colours.

1 Draw a slightly curved vertical line.

2 Starting at the tip, draw a second line that gradually widens from the first line as you reach the bottom.

3 Join the two lines with a slightly rounded quill.

4 Starting two thirds of the way up, draw the right-hand vein.

5 Add the left-hand, slimmer vein.

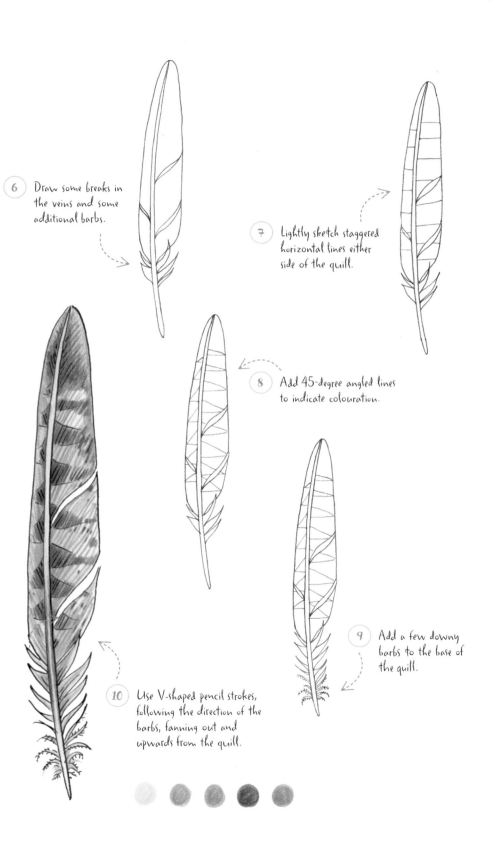

6 Draw some breaks in the veins and some additional barbs.

7 Lightly sketch staggered horizontal lines either side of the quill.

8 Add 45-degree angled lines to indicate colouration.

9 Add a few downy barbs to the base of the quill.

10 Use V-shaped pencil strokes, following the direction of the barbs, fanning out and upwards from the quill.

Woodpecker

There are many different types of woodpecker – try some variations when you've mastered this one.

1 Sketch a diagonal guideline and draw an oval for the head, close to the top.

2 Leaving a small gap, draw a larger oval for the body, then rub out the guideline.

3 Add a beak to the left-hand side of the head and an eye about one quarter of the way across the head.

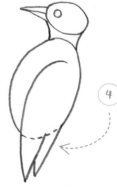

4 Draw the near wing and the tip of the far wing, then rub out any remaining guides.

5 Add the long tail feathers, extending well beyond the tip of the wings.

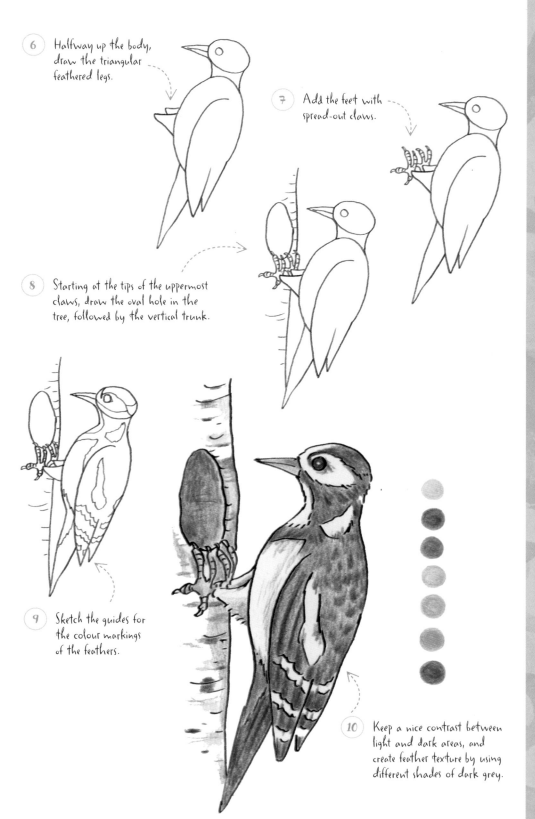

6 Halfway up the body, draw the triangular feathered legs.

7 Add the feet with spread-out claws.

8 Starting at the tips of the uppermost claws, draw the oval hole in the tree, followed by the vertical trunk.

9 Sketch the guides for the colour markings of the feathers.

10 Keep a nice contrast between light and dark areas, and create feather texture by using different shades of dark grey.

Hare

No meadow or field would be complete without this
long-legged, long-eared resident.

1. Draw a diagonal guide with a circle at the top.

2. Add the nose and mouth.

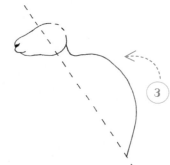

3. Draw a curved line for the back, ending at the dotted line.

4. Sketch the chest, starting from the centre of the lower jaw.

5. Draw a vertical guide on the top of the head and equal in length to the width of the head. Use this to draw the furthest ear, then add the foremost, slightly longer ear at an angle.

6 Position the eye on the diagonal, close to the forehead. Add a bump for the out-of-sight eye, and whiskers. Rub out the diagonal guide.

7 Draw a vertical guide from the chin, then draw the front legs, extending to this line.

8 Rub out the guide and add the back legs.

9 Draw the hare's toes and tail.

10 Use several browns to create a speckled texture to the fur, leave a white highlight around the eye and give the ears black tips.

Coast

Starfish

This classic rockpool resident is the perfect addition to any seashore sketch.

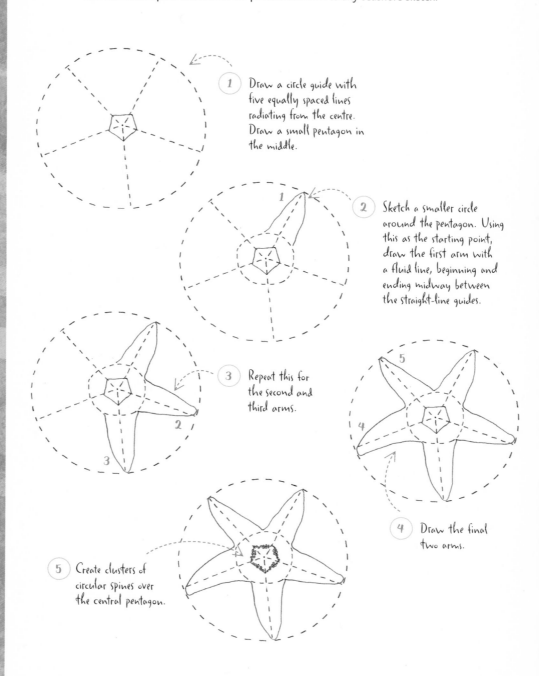

1. Draw a circle guide with five equally spaced lines radiating from the centre. Draw a small pentagon in the middle.

2. Sketch a smaller circle around the pentagon. Using this as the starting point, draw the first arm with a fluid line, beginning and ending midway between the straight-line guides.

3. Repeat this for the second and third arms.

4. Draw the final two arms.

5. Create clusters of circular spines over the central pentagon.

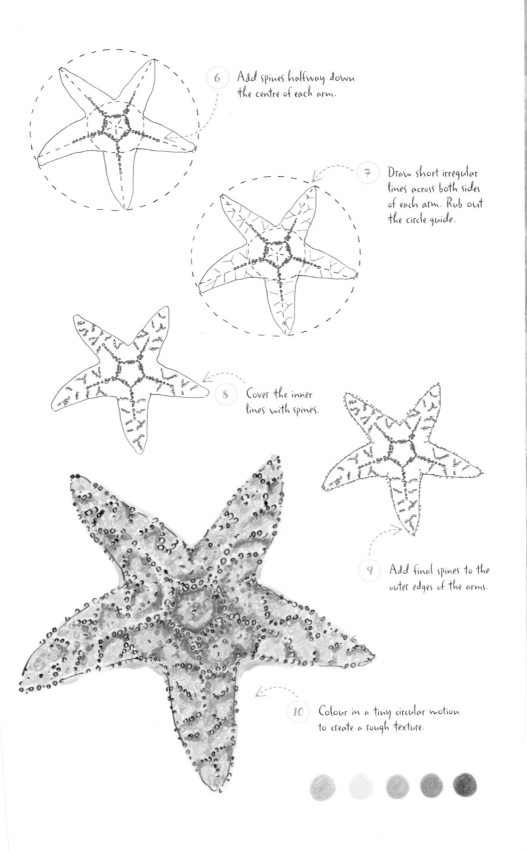

6 Add spines halfway down the centre of each arm.

7 Draw short irregular lines across both sides of each arm. Rub out the circle guide.

8 Cover the inner lines with spines.

9 Add final spines to the outer edges of the arms.

10 Colour in a tiny circular motion to create a rough texture.

Gull

This renowned chip thief can be found swooping over the beaches of the world. Saving your lunch might be difficult but drawing a seagull isn't.

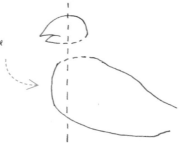

1. Draw an oval with a triangular shape cutting into it.

2. Sketch a guide through the centre of your original shape and create the body.

3. Connect the head to the body with curved lines and rub out the guideline.

4. Draw a beak emerging from the triangular shape on the face, then add a beady eye.

5. Add the wings, creating some feathers at the edge.

6) Give the seagull some long, thin tail feathers.

7) Fill out the tail with more, rounded feathers.

8) Create the legs.

9) Add webbed feet with claws.

10) Use black, white and grey for the body of the bird, then add bright yellow to the beak and pink to the feet.

Crab

Starting with just an oval guide, drawing this crustacean has never been easier.

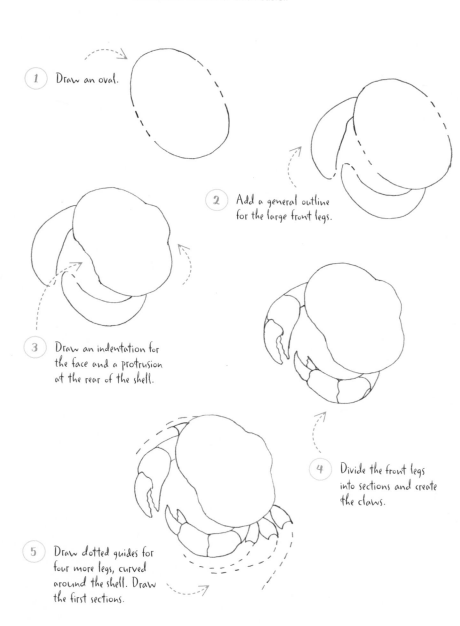

1. Draw an oval.

2. Add a general outline for the large front legs.

3. Draw an indentation for the face and a protrusion at the rear of the shell.

4. Divide the front legs into sections and create the claws.

5. Draw dotted guides for four more legs, curved around the shell. Draw the first sections.

6 Add more sections to the legs.

7 Finish the legs and add a figure-of-eight guide for the rear legs.

8 Draw the rear legs in five sections.

9 Add the eyes and antennae, indentations to the front edge of the shell and spiky hairs on the legs.

10 Use a mix of yellow, orange and red to create the rich texture of the shell. Colour all the ends of the claws black with a white highlight to make them look shiny.

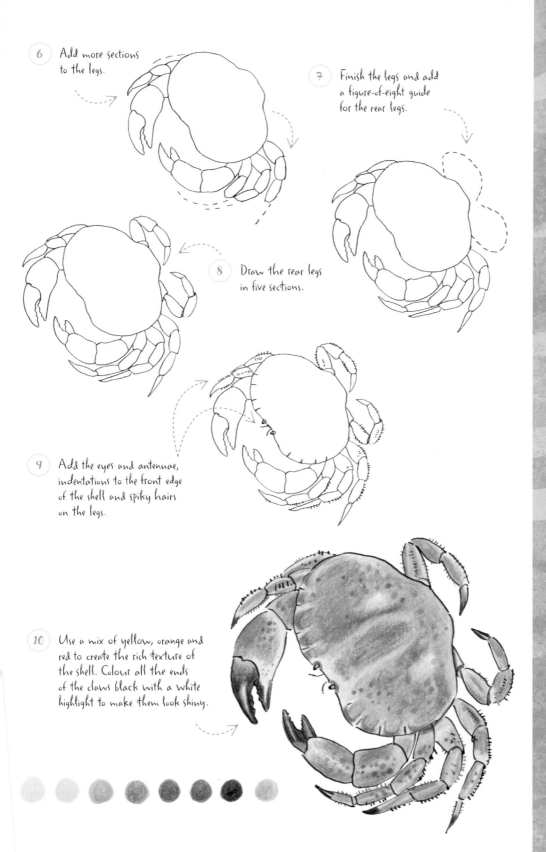

Seaweed

An essential for any underwater scene, seaweed comes in lots of shapes and colours.

1. Draw three branching lines for the midribs.

2. At the top of each line draw a curved V-shape.

3. Draw seven squashed circles for the bladders.

4. Sketch the first blade, following the midrib and joining the Vs at the top.

5. Draw the left-hand blade in the same way.

6. Add the central blade, tucking it behind the two that you have already drawn.

7. Draw an extra blade on the left-hand side.

8. Add a small blade on the right-hand side.

  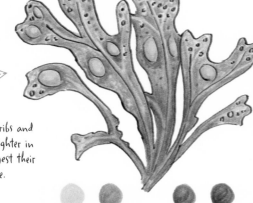

9. Add small dots to suggest the pimpled surface.

10. Keep the midribs and the bladders lighter in colour, to suggest their swollen nature.

Puffin

Puffins are the perfect addition to any ocean scene. Create yours in just a few easy steps.

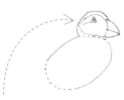
1. Draw a partly dotted tilted oval for the body.

2. Add the head and beak.

3. Sketch in the markings on the face.

4. Draw the eye.

5. Draw the tail and rub out any remaining guidelines.

6. Draw the wing and the feather tips.

7. Add the legs and webbed feet with claws.

8. Create feather markings across the body.

9. Add detail to the beak.

10. Use nice, bright colours for the beak and add plenty of texture to the feathers with lots of shading.

Dolphin

These cheeky characters are a favourite among lovers of marine
life everywhere and they are very easy to draw.

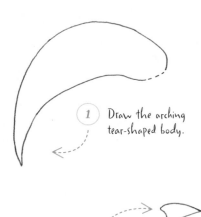

1 Draw the arching
tear-shaped body.

2 Divide the width of the body into quarters with
small dashes. Use the first dash to position a
small eye. Then use the middle dash to draw
the flipper, lining up the top edge.

3 Draw the fin on the
dolphin's back and
the rear flipper.

4 Starting just below the
eye, draw the top smiling
jawline. Next, add the
bottom jaw, protruding
beyond the top jaw.

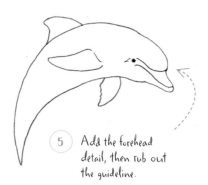

5 Add the forehead
detail, then rub out
the guideline.

6 Draw a splash either side of the dolphin's lower body.

7 Create the tail fin in the water.

8 Add extra droplets to the water.

9 Draw water droplets falling from the dolphin's body.

10 Colour in the dolphin as smoothly as possible to give the impression of glistening skin. Use different shades of blue for the sea and the skin of the dolphin.

Shells

These seaside favourites are the perfect subject for beach lovers everywhere. Follow these steps to draw them with ease.

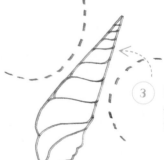

(1) Draw three guides – one diagonal line and two curved lines. Draw a cone shape centred on the diagonal guide.

(2) Add the lip and opening to the first shell.

(3) Draw diagonal sections along the length of the cone.

(4) Create a wide V-shape joining the right-hand dotted arc.

(5) Draw the arc in scallops, then rub out the guide shape.

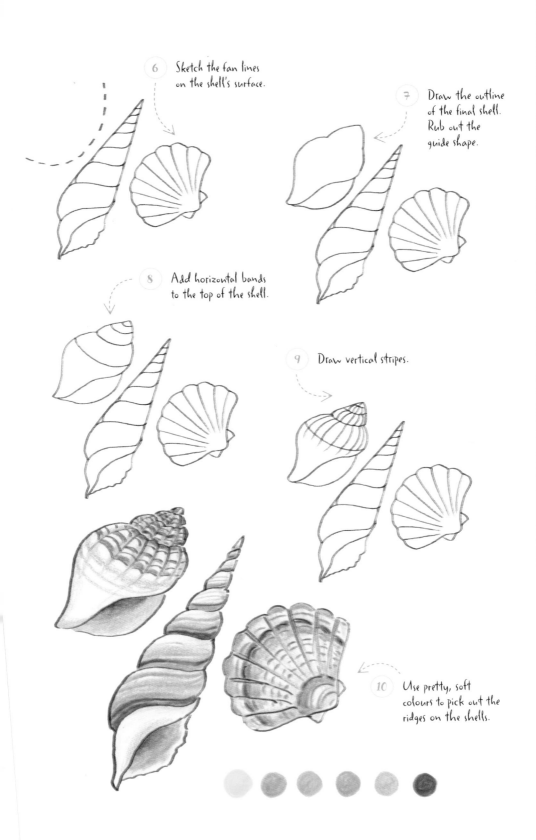

6　Sketch the fan lines on the shell's surface.

7　Draw the outline of the final shell. Rub out the guide shape.

8　Add horizontal bands to the top of the shell.

9　Draw vertical stripes.

10　Use pretty, soft colours to pick out the ridges on the shells.

Turtle

Turtles are fascinating creatures, often migrating long distances to feed. They are also great fun to draw.

1. Draw a squashed oval shape for the body.

2. Draw a diagonal line for the edge of the shell.

3. Add the two visible flippers.

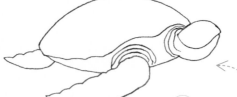

4. Draw the upturned head, rub out the guidelines, then add wrinkles around the neck and flipper joints.

5. Draw the underneath edge of the shell, then the first row of pattern around the shell.

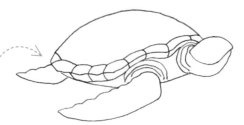

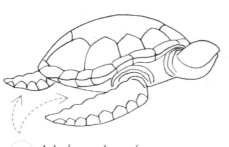

6 Add the second row of
segments on the shell and
those along the lower edge
of the flippers.

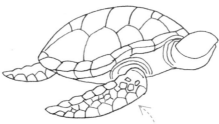

7 Finish the pattern detail on
the shell and front flipper.

8 Draw the downward-slanting
eye so the lower corner lines
up with the lower lip. Sketch
ridges in the sand.

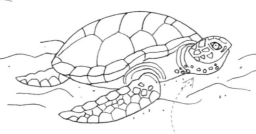

9 Add the final
pattern detail to the
head and neck.

10 Make the gaps between the pattern
segments on the shell pale blue and
on the flippers yellow.

Seal

These marine mammals can be seen in the sea or lounging on the beach.
Use circular shapes to create the round face and eyes.

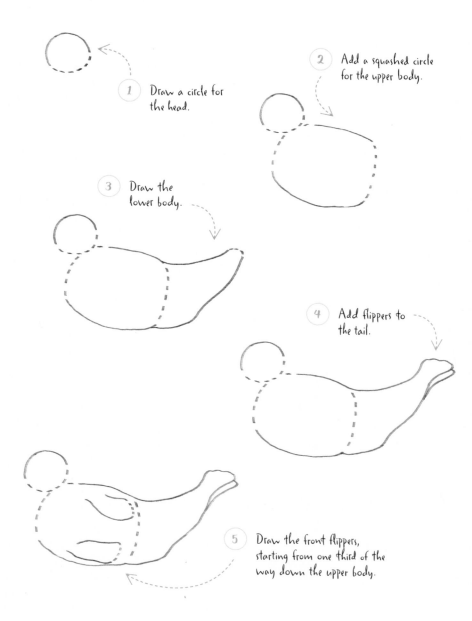

1. Draw a circle for the head.

2. Add a squashed circle for the upper body.

3. Draw the lower body.

4. Add flippers to the tail.

5. Draw the front flippers, starting from one third of the way down the upper body.

6 Add the long claws and draw curves joining the head to the body.

7 In the lower half of the head, draw the muzzle and widely spaced eyes. Rub out the guides.

8 Add the face and fur details.

9 Draw pebbles beneath the seal.

10 Keep the seal's belly quite pale but create darker mottled skin towards the tail.

Hermit crab

These cute crabs often use abandoned sea snail shells to protect their soft bodies. Here, four of the ten legs are hidden in the shell.

1. Draw an ear-shaped curve for the shell.

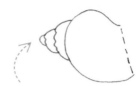

2. Create the tip of the shell by building on top of the curve.

3. Draw the top of the head and two cylindrical eyes. Add a line for the shell opening.

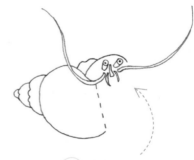

4. Add two short and two long antennae.

5. Draw six leg sections fanning out from the bottom of the face.

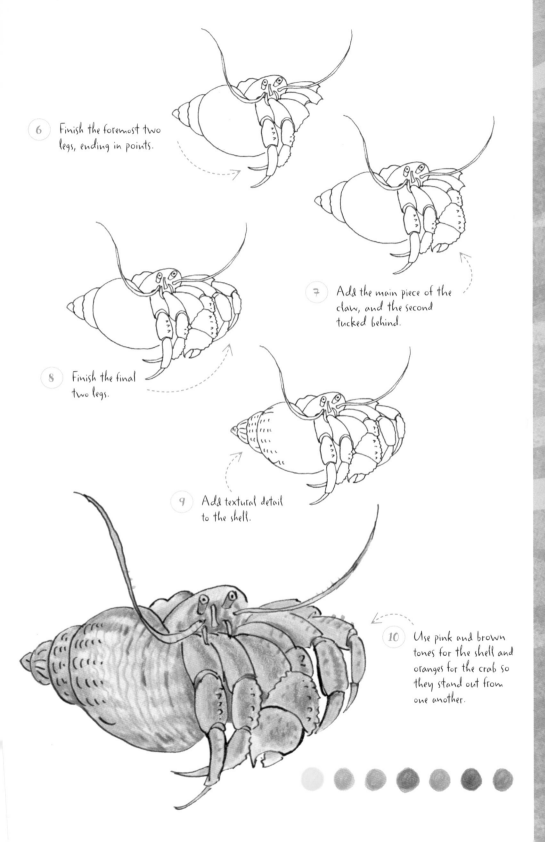

6 Finish the foremost two legs, ending in points.

7 Add the main piece of the claw, and the second tucked behind.

8 Finish the final two legs.

9 Add textural detail to the shell.

10 Use pink and brown tones for the shell and oranges for the crab so they stand out from one another.

Pebbles

You can often see an interesting assortment of pebbles on the beachfront. No two stones are the same, so follow these steps to practise the different shapes and textures.

1 Draw five pebble shapes and a sixth circular guide shape.

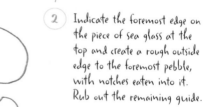

2 Indicate the foremost edge on the piece of sea glass at the top and create a rough outside edge to the foremost pebble, with notches eaten into it. Rub out the remaining guide.

3 Add patches of glaze to the tumbled terracotta tile.

4 Draw criss-cross quartz veining on the far-right pebble.

5 Add stripes wrapping around the central pebble.

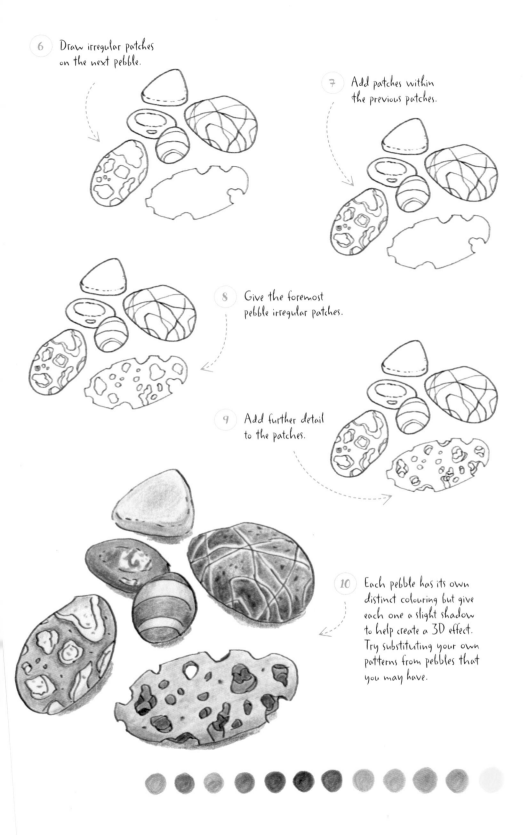

6 Draw irregular patches on the next pebble.

7 Add patches within the previous patches.

8 Give the foremost pebble irregular patches.

9 Add further detail to the patches.

10 Each pebble has its own distinct colouring but give each one a slight shadow to help create a 3D effect. Try substituting your own patterns from pebbles that you may have.

About the artist

Mary Woodin is an artist and illustrator based in Suffolk, UK. She specializes in painting natural subjects and produces artwork for everything from stationery to ceramic tiles. Mary's interest in the outdoors has inspired a number of publications, including *The Painted Garden Cookbook* (a collection of illustrated recipes that were produced in her own garden) and *Drawn to the Country*. Her most recent clients include Waitrose, PepsiCo and the Maybourne Hotel Group.

If you'd like to find out more information or to see further examples of her work, you can visit her website: marywoodin.com

Acknowledgements

Dedicated to my late father-in-law, W. John Martindale, who was a talented illustrator, adept with pen and ink. He would have loved that I retrieved his old dip pen and nibs from the attic, brushed off the dust and got them back into flow for the illustrations in this book.

As ever, I'm very grateful to Lucy, Steph and Alex at The Artworks Illustration Agency for helping with this project.